Limehouse Lil
by
Rozelle Raynes

This story is dedicated to my husband, Dick, without whom the magic years we have spent in Limehouse would never have taken place.

Limehouse Lil

And that small corner of London's
docklands where she ruled supreme...
until Canary Wharf arose

Rozelle Raynes

Castweasel Publishing.
Thoresby Park
Newark, Notts.
NG22 9EP

Limehouse Lil

ISBN 0-9547467-1-6

Published by Castweasel Publishing.
Enquiries, etc, to Thoresby Exhibition Centre
Thoresby Park, Newark, Notts. NG22 9EP.

Designed by Off The Wall Associates
www.offthewallassociates.com

Printed by Oyster Press, Whitstable
01227 772605
sales@oysterpress.co.uk

Acknowledgements

For John Gammons: Thank you for all your support and encouragement during the birth and childhood of 'Limehouse Lil', and for helping to produce such a splendid imprint of my thoughts.

My grateful thanks go to my God-daughter, Susie Haigh, who spent many hours discovering the history of the Parish of Limehouse, and compiling it into a book she wrote for me called "A Profile of Limehouse through six Centuries with particular regard to No. 88 Narrow Street."

CONTENTS

*Overleaf: Our house (the third from left) and Woodward Fisher's Barge Yard. A painting by Charles Napier Hemy circa 1911.

Chapter I

The Rose and Crane

"Good Heavens!" exclaimed Dick, pointing to some big white birds hovering in the sky above us. "I do believe they're seagulls."

"Yes, so they are," I murmured happily as I watched one particular bird glide serenely by on a breath of air, its outstretched wings turned to burnished gold in a fleeting shaft of sunlight.

We were standing on the corner of Ropemakers Fields gazing across the road at a group of shabby old houses hemmed in between a barge repair yard at one end and a small intimate-looking public-house at the other. There were slender clouds with gilded edges sailing across the heavens as if bent on some urgent mission that would brook no delay; and a cluster of dark red chimney-pots, each one imbued with its own distinctive character, arose from the roofs of those venerable dwellings and made sharp clear-cut impressions on the evening sky above them. And just behind us an enormous chimney, known as Limehouse Lil, was belching out wreaths of smoke that drifted away towards the Tower of London.

We had an appointment to view one of the houses across the road at eight o'clock, and I stood there contemplating it for a few minutes, completely enraptured with what I saw. "This is it," I told myself with utter conviction. "The end of the long road is in sight!"

Dick and I were no novices in the matter of house-hunting. Ever since he became a G.P. in a Kentish country town, at the same time as we decided to get married, we had been moving in and out of desirable residences with a certain persistence and regularity. The first place we left because it was too small, and we wanted to try out the REAL countryside; the second one because the birds woke us at 4 A.M., mice came in through the same hole as the telephone wires and Scotch thistles grew in the middle of the sitting-room floor; and the third one because our landlord had a trying habit of lifting our cutlery and playing our favourite records as soon as our backs were turned. But this move was to be the move to end all moves, the ultimate root-establishing transmigration, and we were determined not to make any mistakes this time.

That very afternoon we had been to see a small house in a rather choice cul-de-sac off Greenwich Park. It was just the size we were looking for, it had a discreet garden at the back and the Georgian frontage was quite enchanting; also the price was just right, ominously right it had seemed to me in that pregnant moment when the owner revealed the figure he was asking. I recalled with a shudder the indisputable RIGHTNESS about the whole of that property, and yet the only thing that made a big impression on me was the mammoth size of the television set which dominated the small but elegant drawing-room.

Dick shook me out of my trance and, sensing the dangerous trend of my thoughts, he warned me to keep my mouth shut if we liked this place as it might be necessary to enter into some delicate negotiations with the owner. Wearing his firm-jawed no-nonsense expression, he led the way across the street to the doorstep of Number 88 and boldly rang the bell. As if in answer to his summons, a tug hooted imperiously on the far side of the house. A minute or two later the door was opened by a very tall man with a rugged and rather tragic face. He smiled at us disarmingly and said: "Do come inside; but I may as well tell you before you advance any further, that in my opinion this is the most beautiful house in London!"

Dick and I exchanged significant glances behind his back, and I noticed with alarm that his eyes shone with the light of battle which made them look fiercer and

Seagulls flying over the Narrow Street chimneys.

Narrow Street in the old days.

bluer than usual.

Leading the way through the narrow hall, the owner told us that the row of houses from 78 to 88 Narrow Street had been derelict and scheduled for demolition some six years previously, but he had stepped into the breach and fought a prolonged battle against the G.L.C. and Tower Hamlets Borough Council to save them from destruction. He had stressed the fact that they were amongst the last surviving houses between Tower Bridge and the Isle of Dogs, along the north bank of the river, and his own house, Number 88, had a history of uninterrupted occupation right back to the reign of Queen Elizabeth I. Later on that evening he showed us with pride a photostat of the original lease which was granted by the Wentworths, a famous

Limehouse Lil towering above Brightlingsea Buildings.

The rag and bone man.

Parliamentarian family and the then owners of the Manor of Stebenhythe (later Stepney), to a local shipwright, one "Richard Adames of Rattcliff and his heyres"; and it was to run for five hundred years from 1587 on a peppercorn rent.

At the far end of the hall stood a most amazing vehicle which I took to be a Russian troika at first glance, but we were soon informed by its owner that it was a very rare example of a New England horsedrawn sleigh. I believe it was the sight of that snow-vehicle so soon after we had entered the house that unhinged us at the outset, and made us more susceptible to the quality of unreality and magic which seemed to permeate the whole building.

Leading out of the hall was a very long room which

had rough whitewashed walls, a floor of ancient Devon tiles and three immense oak beams supporting a whitewashed ceiling. The tide was high that evening and the sunlight was dancing on the river close up under the house, some of its reflected glory shimmering on the ceiling of that huge black and white room.

The furnishings consisted of a narrow bed lurking obscurely in one corner, and a number of oil paintings propped against the walls which had certainly been inspired from those very windows. It transpired that this was the 'pad' of a man called Trevor who lived there all the time, whereas the owner spent much of the year travelling in America and elsewhere. Straight away I fell in love with Trevor's pad and began to feel sorry for him as I visualized my leather-topped writing-desk beside the largest window in that glorious room.

A sturdy Dutch coaster slid by, and a cluster of iron

Our house (the third from left) and Woodward Fisher's Barge Yard.

barges, moored just below the windows, clanged together in her wash like distant thunder reverberating through a mountain valley.

We left Trevor's pad and followed the owner up the steep narrow staircase. On the next floor there was a bathroom fit for a Roman Emperor's palace and, on the far side of the passage, a small library with a magnificent fireplace and bookshelves right up to the ceiling on either side. Dick's expression reminded me of the beam of a lighthouse on a dark winter's night as he pictured to himself a roaring log fire in the grate, a pair of soft armchairs in front of it and all his old favourites up on those shelves. The owner, who was an author and historian of no small fame, noted his reactions with pleasure and told us that this was his own favourite room in the whole house, where he had spent more happy hours than anywhere else.

The fourth side of the library opened on to a very large and beautiful apartment. The walls were panelled and painted white, and the floor was laid with ancient pine planks, some of them almost two feet wide, caulked with rope between the seams which gave one the pleasant illusion of being on the deck of a square-rigged sailing-ship. It was rumoured that the house had once belonged to a sail-maker during the heyday of the East and West India Docks, and that room used to be his sail-loft. It faced south across the river, and at the far end was a small balcony enclosed by long windows. It had a splendid view up and down Limehouse Reach and directly across the water to the warehouses guarding Lavender Pond on the Rotherhithe shore.

Old Father Thames was in full spate, a seething torrent of grey-green liquid shot with darts of purest gold. And the flood stream moved emphatically westwards towards London Town, past all the wharves and dock entrances, the ships in ballast and slender cranes, the new tower blocks and the crumbling tenements and riverside pubs.

I had already reached that dangerous stage in the house-buying business when I was mentally placing our own furniture in the most advantageous positions, quite oblivious of the financial pros and cons of the whole matter, or surveyor's reports, exorbitant rates and other dreary details. Fortunately Dick is more level-headed than I am, and he did not allow the thrilling impact of the library to sway his better judgement as we moved upstairs. I noticed him opening up a small but very sharp penknife as we entered the kitchen, and when the owner's back was turned for a few seconds he tried plunging it into an old oak beam that spanned the ceiling. I held my breath, but all was well; Elizabeth 1 oak resisted Elizabeth II steel. No wonder the wooden walls of England were her strength and pride in those bygone days!

The kitchen was the same luxurious size as the bathroom on the floor below, and it commanded an impressive view of Narrow Street and Brightlingsea Buildings, a large block of flats on the far side of Ropemakers Fields; also a miniature public-house called the Black Horse at the far end of the buildings.

On the other side of the second floor landing was a small black room which took us by surprise. It had black William Morris wall-paper, black oak beams, an ugly little black fireplace and black lace curtains over the long French window. The owner told us that this was his bedroom, and he found it essential to sleep in really dark surroundings in order to collect his thoughts properly for the hours of daylight. Hoping that he was not a thought-reader, I began to plan the transformation of that room into a realm of pale grey sunlight, with a Dutch fireplace adorned with Delft tiles.

We passed through the French window on to a large balcony, about twenty-four feet by fourteen, and in the far right-hand corner I saw a scarlet, crimson and golden-coloured rose called Flaming Peace rising up triumphantly out of a cavity in the wall between our balcony and the one next-door. Behind this magnificent bloom was a tall crane outlined against the setting sun, for all the world like some giant giraffe, which dipped its head from time to time to pluck a few bags of coal from the hold of a collier lying alongside the Stepney Power Station wharf. There were scores of seagulls shouting to each other in mid-air, and a solitary bumble-bee buzzing contentedly amongst the horticulture on the neighbour's balcony; and down by the Isle of Dogs an outward-bound tramp steamer blew her siren forlornly in the gathering dusk.

The dreamlike quality of our present surroundings took an even firmer hold. Never before had we viewed a house with such idyllic surprises on every floor, where one seemed utterly incapable of concentrating on the hard facts of life like the position of the boiler or the number of steep winding stairs leading from the ground floor to the top of the house.

We gained that final elevation at last, and found ourselves in another large room panelled in some golden-coloured wood. Through the middle of the floor, like a tree set in the middle of a forest glade, arose the Tudor brick chimney around which the whole house had been built. And as if that was not enough splendour for the last room, there was yet another small balcony facing the sunrise, with the lovable family of chimney-pots I had noticed from Ropemakers Fields commanding the immediate foreground.

That was all. We followed the owner back down the stairs to the library, where he poured out three glasses of sherry and talked to us about American history and French politics and Venezuelan sewers. Three times Dick asked him some highly pertinent question about the house to which he replied on the first two occasions that he had personally been responsible for writing most of Gaitskell's speeches, and on the third one that they were now making a film of his first book and he had been extremely busy that morning selecting the cast. However some trifling mention of the price he was asking did occur in between other irrelevant matters, and it turned out to be more than double that of the one we had seen in Greenwich earlier that afternoon. The owner, however, made a special point of adding that if we should consider buying it he would be grateful if we would promise him never to contemplate reselling without giving him the first option of buying it back.

On that rather sad note we took our leave. Dick, who had plagued me with cautionary warnings beforehand, turned round on the door-step and said to the tall man with the tragic eyes:"Although I'm sure it's the last thing that one should admit at a time like this, but we both agree with you that it really IS the most beautiful house in London!"

The Rose and Crane - looking upriver.

Chapter II

Moving House

It was the nineteenth day of September and all the omens seemed auspicious. On the previous afternoon I had noticed a pure black cat crossing the road briskly from left to right, and that very morning a piebald pony attached to a milk-float had passed across Blackheath, as if by special intervention from above. There was a clear blue sky unsullied by the faintest suspicion of a cloud, and a gentle zephyr whispered among the upper branches of the trees surrounding the Paragon.

We had been packed up and ready to go for seven days or more and I was conscious of a curious tingling sensation in my veins, a premonition of some enormous happiness looming on the near horizon. Dick, who had been working in the Borough of Newham Health

No 88 Narrow Street (in the centre) about the time we moved in.

Two of Mr Fordyce's 'little limbs of Satan', offering to help unload. *see p22.*

Department for the past year or so, set off for his office at nine o'clock. After his departure I lingered on the front door-steps surveying the ever peaceful landscape of Blackheath with mixed emotions. Suddenly a huge pantechnicon from Jordan and Jarrett's removal and storage firm in Canterbury pulled up in front of me, and there was no more time for day-dreaming.

The men who burst out of the van were all old friends. They had stored half our possessions for the past two or three years and moved us no less than six times, and they were in the habit of making rapid and audible assessments of the merits or otherwise of our various changes of address. I sometimes wondered on what system they worked, and I came to the conclusion it must come under two headings; first and foremost, the height of the dwelling and type of staircase they would have to negotiate with our more tiresome bits of furniture; and, secondly, the respectability of the neighbourhood (Blackheath, which we were just about to leave, rated highly in this respect).

For one whole year we had lived in a very small flat under the eaves of the Paragon, which is classified as a historic building, Category I, of quite exceptional beauty. When we first moved to Blackheath many of our friends and relations had breathed a sigh of relief, for at last, they felt, we were going to settle down in reputable surroundings. And some of them managed to recall a favourite grandparent, great-aunt or cousin who had once lived in a charming old house overlooking the heath. All that was very gratifying, and no one can deny that Blackheath is a fine open part of London where the air is fresher and the houses more attractive than in many other districts. But it was not for us; we had lived in East London for a year before our Blackheath period, and we both had an overwhelming desire to return there.

Well, we were on our way back to the north side of the river now, and I was filled with a great surge of excitement; also a slightly guilty sensation of relief at leaving behind all those prohibitive notices: "Private Property", "Do not park here", "Keep off the Grass", "Dogs not allowed in this garden which is solely for the inhabitants of the Paragon" and so on, ad infinitum. Nearby lived my special 'bête noire', an old woman who threw up her window whenever she saw me exercising our Airedale bitch, Texel, in the enormous garden belonging to all who lived in those flats.

"Don't let that horrid brute of yours foul the grass," she would screech at me; "or I shall report you to the Garden Committee."

She did too, and a few days later I was approached by a formidable gentlewoman wearing a Scotch tweed tailor and sensible crepe-soled shoes, who told me that our dog was only permitted to use the garden if she did nothing of a serious nature whilst she was in it. Immediately I spotted a flaw in this arrangement as the garden was about half a mile long with entrances at either end, so I asked her what action I should take if the dog was taken short in mid-garden, so to speak? Evidently the humour of that possible situation did not appeal to her, for she changed the subject abruptly and said that she had had a further complaint from Mrs B. on the ground floor, who had been forced to take her cat to an animal's psychiatrist because our dog had looked at it through the window on three occasions and, apparently, sent it into a gibbering decline.

On that September morning I sped down the motorway leading into the Blackwall Tunnel, and as I drove I sang at the top of my voice a little song which I had just invented called "Seagulls over Stepney".

The pantechnicon and I arrived in Narrow Street simultaneously, and I noticed Mr Fordyce, the Storage Manager, who had particularly asked to be included on this removal, looking rather dubiously up and down the street. A lorry-driver emerged from the entrance to a yard a few doors away from Number 88 and shouted to the driver of the van: "Ang on Mate, till I've shifted this load'o'timber, then you can git yer van in alongside o' the 'ouse."

This gesture of friendliness from the first native they had met caused the men to look more cheerful, and despite the fact that both Points 1 and 2 in their assessment of our latest home were obviously going to be unsatisfactory, the driver began to whistle the opening bars of "Cruising down the River".

I fitted the key into the front door of Number 88 and turned it with some trepidation. At that moment our dog pushed past me and ran down the length of the hall, sniffing avidly to right and left, then turned into Trevor's pad and made a thorough investigation of the whole room. By the time I caught up with her I saw that her tail was elevated at an angle of 200^0 and wagging gently, and her ears were arranged in certain soft contours which usually signified approval of her surroundings.

Mr Fordyce had followed close behind me "to size up the job", as he put it, pointing out to me in a severe manner that he had left the others in the van to guard the contents as you never knew what might happen up in London, did you? I applauded his cautious forethought and led the way up the narrow winding staircase. The sun was streaming in across the pine-planked floor of the sitting-room and there were undulating patterns of light and shade dancing on the broad white ceiling. Beyond the window the gleaming river slapped playfully against the iron hulls of the barges moored outside Woodward Fisher's yard, and bits of flotsam and jetsam moved downstream on the ebb, bound for who knows what exciting destinations.

Mr Fordyce dropped his businesslike manner as he surveyed the library and sitting-room. "Most unexpected," he announced admiringly, "especially after you've had a decko at the outside of the place." I tried to say something soothing about the outside but he wasn't really listening. "We'll soon have all those boxes of books unpacked and up on those shelves," he continued enthusiastically. "And that little old bit of oak furniture what you used to have on the left of the fireplace at Pluckley would just fit in lovely in that corner."

A favourite picture above the bathroom mantlepiece.

A Croatian 'brazzera', made for us by Matko Bonačeić-Protty at Milna on the Island of Brač.

I was astonished to find that Mr Fordyce remembered the exact position occupied by our various bits of furniture in our last home but two, and had already decided where they should stand in our latest one. However I agreed with all his proposals cheerfully, thinking that I should certainly have to re-arrange all the books after his departure.

The staircase proved a real problem, and by the time Dick arrived for a brief visit during his lunch hour, our sofa was firmly wedged in the sharp corner leading to the first floor landing; and his favourite chest-of-drawers was attached to a bight of rope suspended from a gantry which had been rigged out of the kitchen window on the second floor, and it was describing gentle semicircles in mid-air some twenty feet above the heavy lorry traffic passing along Narrow Street. The kettle had just come to the boil and I was busy pouring out tea for everyone, without quite realizing that no one was in a position to drink it. Either they were stuck the wrong side of the sofa like Dick, or they were much too busy supervising the aerial manoeuvres of his chest-of-drawers.

However, with all such dilemmas they have a way of sorting themselves out if

one remains quite calm. Dick made good use of the time by

fetching a few bottles of beer from a little public-house called The Grapes, six doors along, and by the time he returned the stair-case was no longer blocked and his chest-of-drawers had set off on the second stage of its journey; out through the previous owner's small black bedroom on to the main balcony; and then up into the air on the river side of the house, in order to make its final entry into the

Grandpa's beautiful picture of the Nun.

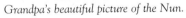
Top: Unloading: our possessions, hauling them in through the kitchen windows.

main bedroom window on the top floor.

Once this feat had been safely accomplished Mr Fordyce called a halt, and we moved out on to the balcony where Dick was busy opening bottles of beer. One of the gang, a huge man with arms as broad and solid as oak trees, raised his glass and, wishing us good luck in our new home, he observed; "This is the third bloomin' historic monument we've moved

Dick painting the front door.

you into, and next time how about choosin' a nice little modern bungalow on the outskirts of Canterbury!"

We laughed and said we hoped there wasn't going to be a next time, whereupon Mr Fordyce looked rather crestfallen and said he was going to miss all our furniture as his store looked quite empty and deserted without it.

A few minutes later Dick returned to his office and the men unlocked their van and started unloading again. In the meantime five small children, who had been keeping an eye on the house for some time, ventured across the road and accosted Mr Fordyce: "Can we give you a 'and, Mister; to carry somefink inte the 'ouse?"

Their spokesman was a little dark-eyed girl of about eight, and Mr Fordyce explained to her in a serious manner that it was against Union rules to let anyone else touch what came out of their van. The girl nodded her understanding but her small brother, who was several years younger, looked as if he might burst into tears. However, they hung around hopefully and before long they had set up a miniature encampment on the sloping ramp of the van which did not make it any easier for the men to extract some of our larger pieces of furniture. I overheard Mr Fordyce muttering something about 'little limbs of Satan' as I passed him on the stairs.

My piano had just negotiated the journey from the van to Trevor's pad, and a crate of kitchen utensils was swinging dizzily about in mid-air when I heard a man's voice on the other side of the house. I went out on to the balcony just in time to see an old Thames sailing-barge running before the gentle breeze towards Wapping with only two men aboard her, one at the helm and the other one bending over the anchor winch in a purposeful manner.

Dick came home from work soon after five o'clock and the men were still busy unpacking seemingly endless crates

Dick and me on the lower balcony.
Opposite, The Thames sailing barge sailing gently by.

of crockery, glassware, books, blankets and curtains. The sun had already set behind Tower Bridge by the time they had finished and we all sat down to one final pot of tea.

"The best of British luck to you!" called out Mr Fordyce as the van backed into Ropemakers Fields, then set off eastwards on its long journey home.

Dick and I stood on the doorstep for a few minutes after they had gone, gazing up and down the street. A man came out of the Black Horse along at the end of Ropemakers Fields, and he held the door ajar for a few seconds whilst he turned to say goodnight to his mates. I caught a fleeting glimpse of a smoky little bar with someone bent double over an old honky-tonk piano, attacking the keyboard in a forceful way. Beside him stood a buxom woman wearing a black sequin blouse over a tight black skirt, with platinum-blonde hair piled dramatically on top of her head. Her mouth was wide open and out of her throat, her heart, her whole being poured an old Cockney song. It was harsh and earth-shattering and funny and sad; as if she was the mouthpiece of all the Cockney singers in creation:-

"Orff went the cart wiv me 'ome packed in it,
I walked be'ind wiv me ole cock linnet
But I dil-lied and dal-lied, dal-lied and I dil-lied..."

Just then the door swung to and all the part about the old-time copper was soft and muted, like the tones of twilight after a sunset of spectacular glory.

Chapter III

The Sailor's Parish

It was the magic hour in Limehouse Reach, the time of the afterglow, when the harsh sounds and colours of the daytime had mellowed into a soft harmony, a vague mysterious world inhabited by creatures of fantasy. The rusty iron barges aground on the shingle became sleeping leviathans from some bygone age, and a Scandinavian timber ship plodding upriver against the last of the ebb was transformed into a quinquereme of Nineveh with a cargo of ivory, apes and peacocks, sandlewood, cedarwood and sweet white wine.

I sat in a corner of the balcony day-dreaming about the time when Limehouse used to be a famous seafaring neighbourhood; and I felt entirely at peace with the world as I watched a seagull take off from the deck of a barge on the foreshore and hover in the purple dusk a few feet away from me, a pale phantom bird dimly outlined against the evening river.

It was during the reign of Queen Elizabeth I that the history of Limehouse first revealed a definite association with the world of maritime affairs. Those two famous half-brothers, Sir Walter Raleigh and Sir Humphrey Gilbert, were both known to have lived in Narrow Street at some period during their dazzling careers; in fact the previous owner of our house had been at great pains to prove to us that it was the actual building in which the greatest of all Elizabethan adventurers had stayed before he set sail on his third voyage to Guiana on a pinnace called the "Watte".

Although we have never been able to substantiate this, the very atmosphere of the place seemed to whisper of splendid deeds upon the high seas, and it did not take a wide stretch of the imagination to picture ourselves sharing the balcony with one of Queen Elizabeth's favourite courtiers.

Sir Martin Frobisher, Sir Hugh Willoughby and

Top: The harbour-master's house in Narrow Street.
Bottom: The Isle of Dogs in the 19th Century, with many tall ships in the docks.

Stephen and William Borough all embarked on their voyages of exploration from Ratcliffe Cross Stairs along at the western end of Narrow Street. Those same worn old steps still ran down into the river between two immense dark warehouses, a constant reminder of the brave seafarers of bygone days; and also some of the criminals leaving for the colonies.

Phineas Pett, one of the most celebrated shipwrights of his century, built the "Greyhound" at Duke Shore Wharf in 1586. By leaning well out over our balcony we could just see the end of the slipway from which that fine old vessel was launched into the Thames, more than four hundred years ago. And James Welsh, the captain of the "Richard of Arundel", was reported to have dropped anchor just off there in 1591 in order to discharge a cargo of 587 sacks of pepper, 150 elephant's teeth and 32 barrels of oil of palm trees.

In a later century Captain Cook married a Shadwell girl at St. Paul's Church in the Ratcliffe Highway, and thereafter Shadwell became his home parish to which he always returned on his fleeting visits to this country. And then there was Captain Bligh aboard H.M.S. "Bounty", who set sail from Free Trade Wharf close to Ratcliffe Cross Stairs in 1787.

Despite all those illustrious seamen who embarked from this reach of the river several centuries ago, it was not until the opening of the East and West India Docks at the beginning of the nineteenth century that Limehouse reached its pinnacle of fame. As a seafaring neighbourhood it became renowned amongst sailors from the furthest corners of the globe. Many Chinamen and Lascars, who first arrived in London aboard Duncan Dunbar's East Indiamen, deserted their ships and settled down in Limehouse during that period; and it was not long before a flourishing Chinatown had been established around the junction of the East and West India Dock Roads. A network of small streets with Oriental names sprang up like mushrooms; there was Peking Street, Canton Street, Amoy Place, Malabar Street, Nankin Street, Oriental Street and Mandarin Street; but perhaps the two best known ones were Pennyfields and Limehouse Causeway, which runs into Narrow Street. Despite the bombing of the East End during the Second World War, most of those streets still remain. Some are now adorned with blocks of council flats or rows of smart maisonettes but, here and there, it is still possible to conceive a picture of the old Chinatown as it must have been in the nineteenth century. The streets were narrower in those days, and lined with slender dark brick houses which jostled each other for breathing-space; and the people inside those picturesque dwellings struggled for living-room in an atmosphere that was smoky and fetid.

There were chop-suey joints, sailor's pubs and boarding-houses, marine stores and tattoo parlours, seamen's outfitters and a medley of small shops which sold satsumas and brassware, whale's teeth and shells, exotic silk garments and Oriental food. And along the Ratcliffe Highway one could find shops selling wild beasts brought back by sailors from remote parts of the world.

Great celebrations took place in Limehouse at the time of the Chinese New Year. Garlands of strangely-fashioned coloured lanterns hung across the streets, and the noise of exploding fire-crackers rent the still night air in the heart of Docklands. The mah-jong players rattled their miniature bricks until the early hours of the morning, and all the cooks were busy preparing mountains of food for the Feast of the Lanterns.

Behind the main streets there was a warren of alleyways where seamen fought each other with sharp knives, and opium dens and brothels abounded. The Chinese settlers, however, kept very much to themselves and rarely made trouble with their English neighbours. Amongst the local inhabitants the men had the reputation of being good husbands and kind fathers, and the sinister aura with which Limehouse was invested during the Victorian age was largely inspired by a few popular novelists who had discovered that Chinatown was a suitably romantic setting for their murky plots. Mr Watts, the rector of St. Anne's Church, and old Pop, the ninety-year-old father of the landlady of The Grapes, were both liable to vouch for this fact in the most forceful manner when they were questioned about the vicious inhabitants of that area by some apprehensive tourists from the West End.

The growth of prosperity among the tall clipper ships racing home with tea from China, and later on with wool from Australia, was strongly reflected in the fortunes of Limehouse. London River must have been a splendid sight around 1860; the Pool of London and the docks were crammed full of ships, the masts of which seemed to reach right up to the clouds in the sky, while immense white sails were constantly being hoisted to dry in the sunshine.

Ashore the scene was no less animated. The pavements were crowded with seamen from all parts of the world:

Norwegians, Finns, Germans – the tall blond sons of Northern Europe mingled with the dark-skinned Lascars, the secretive Chinese and harsh-voiced Arabs from the Middle East. Then there were the Southern Europeans – the Spaniards, Portuguese, Italians and Greeks. They might often be seen walking arm-in-arm with local girls who displayed prominent curves and startling hair styles. Irish dockers argued fiercely with burly lumpers, that unique breed of men who handled all the timber in the West India Docks. They worked under the aegis of a public-house, the publican making himself responsible for finding them employment and paying their wages, partly in liquor; so that one rarely encountered a sober lumper!

A delightful description of Narrow Street, written by Christina Black in the nineteenth century, gives one a quite different impression of Limehouse – the part that backs on to the Thames:

"The houses on the south side of Narrow Street look out upon the river. Many of them have bow windows and little wooden balconies, and steps running down into the water. Some of the rooms are low and small, and have about them an odd suggestion of a ship's cabin. As we go down the wooden stairs the blue stretch of the river spreads before us ...."

When dusk fell over Sailorland the gas lamps flickered dimly in the narrow streets, while the strains of some haunting melody being picked out on an old honky-tonk piano would come drifting out into the throbbing Limehouse night. A reddish-golden glow escaped through the thin curtains drawn across some tavern window, an infinitely coaxing sight to a stranger still abroad in the dark tortuous alleyways.

Inevitably those cosmopolitan bands of seamen, newly arrived from braving the dangers of the deep, were drawn as if by some irresistible magnetism into those warm and cheerful public-houses; and they were the places which were remembered with nostalgia on a dark and stormy night at sea or in some God-forsaken hole on the far side of the world, many months or years later.

There was a curious little tale which came drifting back into my memory as I sat day-dreaming in the corner of our balcony. It was about the mate of a tramp-steamer who was sweltering in the heat outside some evil-smelling tavern on the waterfront in Calcutta, and suddenly he was overcome by a fierce pang of homesickness. He sighed deeply and muttered unhappily to himself; "Gawd, for a whiff of Li'mus Reach!"

And lo and behold, a chirpy kind of voice behind him said, "Amen".

The Two Brewers in Narrow Street was one of the most popular pubs for sailors in the early days, where the music was lively and the girls were friendly; then there was The Blue Posts in the West India Dock Road and not far from there, The Star of India and The Cape of Good Hope, all highly-favoured drinking establishments. But towards the end of the nineteenth century Charlie Brown's had become world-famous and swept all the neighbouring public-houses into comparative insignificance. It stood on a corner opposite to the entrance of the West India Docks and for many years its real name was The Railway Tavern, but no seaman would recognise it by any other name than that of its original landlord.

Charlie Brown was a seaman himself for the first half of his life, and when he decided to swallow the anchor and become the licensee of an East End pub he set about turning the whole place into a unique nautical museum. Shark's backbones, stuffed flying-fish, ship's figureheads, tusks of sea-elephants

and a thousand other extraordinary mementoes of his voyages decorated the spacious bars and dance-hall; and it was not long before this remarkable man became known as the uncrowned King of Limehouse. He was said to have given a great deal of money to charity, and one of his favourite maxims was "A sailor should always have a full pot!"

The beginning of the twentieth century heralded a new era in Limehouse. Devastating changes were taking place in the world of maritime affairs, which inevitably had their repercussions in the old seafaring quarters. The great days of the square-rigged sailing-ships were over, and steam-ships were rapidly replacing them in most parts of the civilized world. Those vast new floating leviathans tended to use the Victoria and Albert Docks in North Woolwich more and more, whereas the East and West India Docks had always been the home from home of the windjammer.

Later on, the bad times came when there was a slump

Above: Charlie Brown's, a famous pub on the West India Dock Road.

32

in shipping and a huge surplus of unemployed seamen drifting aimlessly about the streets. Those who could no longer afford a bed in Jack's Palace, the seamen's hotel in Limehouse, or some cheap boarding-house, would sleep on benches in the parks and churchyards or in one of the tunnels under the Thames on a rainy night. During the daytime they could be observed in their hundreds all over Docklands. Some played billiards in the Seamen's Mission in the East India Dock Road; others turned the pages of magazines in the Seamen's Home in Dock Street, their eyes unseeing and their minds unheeding; but the vast majority just stood around outside the Stack of Bricks, Jack's Palace or Green's Home, waiting hopefully for something to turn up and talking, endlessly, about the good old days before the slump.

All day long and half the night they stood there reminiscing about old ships and tough skippers, about stormy days at sea and boisterous nights in harbour. They did not catch the eye, those shabby stranded sons of the sea; rather they seemed to merge with the Limehouse background. The traffic rumbled past and the dark clouds moved purposefully across the smoky London sky; meanwhile they waited patiently for that rare reward – another job afloat.

The masts and funnels of the silent ships rose above the dock walls each night like ghostly apparitions, and mingled with the goblin chimneys of Chinatown. A siren called plaintively from somewhere downriver, and the drunks snored contentedly in the cells of Limehouse Police Station.

There were a number of different aspects of the

Limehouse scene during the early part of the twentieth century. In 1912 Sir Walter Besant wrote a vivid description of it in his fascinating book, "East London":

"After Ratcliffe we pass into Limehouse. It was at Limehouse that Rogue Riderhood lived. The whole place is more marine than Wapping. The public-houses have a look, an air, a something that suggests the seas. The shops are conducted for the wants of the merchantmen; the houses are old and picturesquely dirty; the streets are narrow; one may walk about these streets for a whole afternoon, and find something to observe in everyone, either a shop full of queer things or a public-house full of strange men, or a house that speaks of other days – of crimps, for instance, and of press gangs, and of encounters in the streets; there are ancient docks used for the repair of wooden sailing-ships; there are places where they build barges; a little inland you may see the famous church of Limehouse, with its lofty steeple; it was only built in 1730. Before that time there was no church at Limehouse; since that time nobody has gone to church at Limehouse, speaking of the true natives, the riverside folk, not of those who dwell respectably in the West India Dock Road. It is, however, doubtless a great advantage and benefit to a sea-going population to have a churchyard to be buried in."

Despite Sir Walter Besant's caustic remarks about the church-goers of Limehouse, there is still a community spirit in this remote corner of Docklands which approaches the old village ideal. Whether they go to church or not, there is no doubt that St. Anne's Church and Cyril Jackson School are the two focal points in the village of Limehouse, casting their influence over the long-established villagers and the transient flotsam and jetsam without discrimination, like the warm compassionate rays of the sun.

The history of how that historic place of worship first came into being is not without interest. In 1711 an Act of Parliament was passed to authorize an increased duty on all coal arriving in London by river; and the income was to be used to finance the building of those churches on the outskirts of the City where, owing to the huge increase of population, many people were left in spiritual destitution.

Nicholas Hawksmoor, who studied under Sir Christopher Wren and assisted him in the building of St. Paul's Cathedral, was the architect of St. Anne's, as well as two other famous churches in East London, St. George-in-the-East, Shadwell, and Christ Church, Spitalfields. The church in Limehouse took fourteen years to build. Designed in the baroque style which was fashionable at that time, it was an immense and beautifully proportioned building with seating to accomodate no less than fifteen hundred people. Hawksmoor was renowned for his ornate ceilings and the magnificence of his towers, and St. Anne's was no exception to the rule. Rising skywards in

Above: Dick walking towards St Anne's Church.

diminishing white tiers, it soars above the black roofs and chimney-pots of Limehouse, a splendid and inspiring vision to all the puny mortals on the earth below. At the beginning of the nineteenth century, J.P. Nalcolin, in his book "Londinium Redivivum", described it in a most lyrical fashion: "This strange jumble of architecture has a majestic outline; a sailor might be deceived by a distant view, in supposing it a very large ship coming towards him under easy sail, with a flag flying at her main-top."

Because St. Anne's is marked on the Admiralty charts as a navigational landmark, it is one of the few churches in England permitted to fly the White Ensign from its flagpole. It was also the church registry for all children born at sea. The church was consecrated in 1730, and from that time onwards Limehouse ceased to be a hamlet of St. Dunstan's but became a separate parish with its own local government which was responsible for the poor and general rates. The poor rates in those days were considerable and the workhouse and its adjacent school were amongst the largest in the country. Many people believed that Charles Dickens had used the former as an example for his famous workhouse in "Oliver Twist", although he vehemently denied this rumour in a letter he subsequently wrote to the parish beadle. However he often came to Limehouse to visit his godfather, Christopher Huffam, who was a superintendent rigger at a small Admiralty dock in Narrow Street, and lived nearby in Newell Street; so it seems reasonable to suppose that he may have found time to investigate the local school and workhouse, and to have noted the deplorable conditions under which the Limehouse orphans were nurtured.

In 1850 the interior of St. Anne's was completely destroyed by fire, but thanks to the tireless efforts of one of the curates, funds were soon raised for the rebuilding of the church with certain Victorian additions which included a magnificent organ, bought for £800 after it had won first prize at the Great Exhibition in Hyde Park in 1851.

Miraculously St. Anne's was not hit by the bombs which obliterated so much of Docklands during the Second World War. The white steeple which looks like a large ship under easy sail still soars above the Limehouse chimney-pots, whilst down below in the church-yard tattered tramps and meths-drinkers sit around on the wooden benches or lie on their backs on the grass watching the clouds sail by.

Chapter IV

Friday Morning

There were long golden sunbeams streaming through a narrow gap at the top of the curtains, and I lay on my back trying to count a hundred thousand iridescent atoms which were dancing up and down those brilliant paths of light. I had been awakened some while earlier by the unusual noise of a wedge of swans flying across our roof towards the rising sun; and then there were the ship's sirens, urgently demanding the attention of some sleepy dock-master, and seagulls calling to each other in plaintive early morning tones.

I must have dropped off to sleep again for a few minutes; then, quite suddenly, I opened my eyes wide and focussed them on a man wearing a beige raincoat and a brown trilby

Dawn - looking east towards the Isle of Dogs.

hat, who was framed in the doorway leading on to the small balcony which runs along one side of our bedroom. My first reaction was one of intense surprise, to think that Dick should be up and fully dressed so early in the morning. But a moment later I glanced out of the corner of my left eye and saw that he was fast asleep in the bed beside me; and just beyond him I caught a glimpse of our Airedale, Texel, lying on her back in her basket with all four paws waving gently in the air and the sound of heavy breathing coming from her furry nostrils.

"Useless silly dog," I thought to myself furiously. "We might all be murdered in our beds for all she cares! She's certainly not worth her keep."

Having relieved myself of those sentiments, I began to feel exceedingly frightened. The figure in the doorway had moved further along the balcony until he was out of sight behind the curtain, and I could hear two male voices muttering together outside.

I raised myself on one elbow, put my left hand firmly across Dick's mouth to muffle any sudden exclamation he might feel inclined to make, and shook him hard with the other hand. He emerged slowly from a deep and peaceful sleep, half opened one eyelid and regarded me with a slightly pained expression on his face. I then pointed dramatically towards the balcony door with the hand which was not engaged in gripping his mouth, but as this only revealed the usual early morning vista of distant cranes and chimneys on the Isle of Dogs, the significance of my gesture was completely lost on the newly-awakened man beside me.

The voices on the balcony, however, continued their conversation in hoarse whispers, and Dick slowly became aware of this unaccustomed sound. He shook my hand free from his mouth, crawled sleepily out of bed and advanced towards the balcony door like cannon-fodder, as he told people afterwards! I brought up the rear, holding one high-heeled shoe as a weapon and feeling extremely courageous behind the broad shield of my husband's back.

At this juncture the whole dramatic incident turned to pure farce. Dick put a tousled head round the balcony door, expecting to find at least a couple of masked gunmen lurking behind the chimney-pots, but instead he was greeted by a pleasant-looking policeman who wished him a very good morning and said we could go back to bed now as everything was under control. The man in the raincoat and trilby hat was poised at the top of a long ladder which reached right up to the roof of Number 90, the house next door, and it transpired that he was a plain-clothes policeman who had come along to support his friend. They had received an urgent telephone call from a householder further along Narrow Street, who claimed that strange footsteps could be heard tramping about overhead; but they had searched the roof-tops all the way from The Grapes to Duncan Dunbar's Wharf, and had found no traces of this mysterious prowler.

We retired to bed rather sheepishly, and Texel's heavy breathing continued to fill the room with the steady rhythm of an animal without a care in the world.

At seven o'clock the lorry traffic began its daily serenade; a deep monotonous throbbing of powerful engines which might have been the roar of the surf on some distant rock-strewn shore. One of the strangest things about this house is the way the river traffic always sounds as

A warehouse in Limehouse Cut at high water.

if it is steaming along Narrow Street, whilst the road traffic appears to be approaching by way of Limehouse Reach! We have never been able to discover what creates this extraordinary illusion.

Dick opened the curtains, tapped the barometer which was high and rising, then went downstairs to put on the kettle. The sun had risen above the roof-tops and it was streaming through a dark ravine formed by two pairs of chimney-pots which I have christened Lucy and George, and Doris and Albert. One section of the room was flooded with golden avenues of light and down below the river reflected the glory of the morning sky in its fast-flowing waters, causing the ceiling to shimmer with gold and silver ripples. The tide was still ebbing and a solitary beachcomber appeared near some grounded lighters, bent double in his diligent search for half-buried treasures. A year or two ago someone had found a golden sovereign down there, and ever since that day the competition has been fierce among the local mudlarks.

Soon after nine o'clock Dick left for work and I started to sweep up some of the dust which had accumulated just inside the front door. I was on my hands and knees brushing a small heap of dirt into the dustpan, when I noticed the letter-box flap rising slowly and silently to reveal a pair of very round blue eyes which gazed at me with intense interest. I blew out my cheeks in the shape of a balloon and squeezed them between the palms of my hands until they exploded; this caused some high-pitched squeaks on the other side of the door and the sound of several miniature pairs of feet beating a hasty retreat along the narrow pavement.

A few minutes later the telephone rang peremptorily. I

Our view of the neighbouring chimney-pots Lucy, George, Doris and Albert (on the right).

Our dog, Texel.

ran upstairs and lifted the receiver, at the same time wishing that the instrument had never been invented; and the next moment I was desperately trying to devise an excuse to avoid lunching with an old friend of my mother's at a fashionable restaurant in Mayfair. I mumbled some insincere words about being terribly disappointed that I couldn't come but I really was FAR too busy, what with one thing and another. The voice at the other end of the line sounded unconvinced and peevish, and inquired rather testily: "How can you stand living in that ghastly place, MILES away from anywhere?"

My mother, who had an ingenious way of glossing over any unpalatable details and making the most riveting statements which are not always strictly accurate, had recently revealed to some of her friends that her daughter and son-in-law now lived in the City, in a charming old house which once belonged to Sir Walter Raleigh. This announcement caused a certain stir of interest, and a few of them intimated their intention of calling on us soon .... until they looked us up in their A to Zs and discovered that far from being inside the safe and respectable precincts of the City, Narrow Street was very definitely FARTHER EAST, somewhere inside that unplumbed jungle of slumland known as the "East End".

I usually found there was no satisfactory answer to questions like the one I had been asked that morning, for how could I explain to that lady of small understanding that the sun was shining on the river and the flood tide had just started to make, bringing with it heaven knows what exciting cargoes from across the sea; and on the other side of the house there were some tall new blocks of flats beside a very old farmhouse – imagine a farmhouse in the heart of London – and a marvellous white church steeple, distinctly outlined against the pale blue sky. Altogether the horizons seemed broader and the air more invigorating than it did in any other part of London, and there was some special ingredient in the atmosphere which made one feel intensely alive, an impression I had seldom achieved amongst the crowded shops and restaurants of the West End.

When I had finished cleaning the house I set off on a shopping expedition with Texel. We walked eastwards along Narrow Street and as we drew abreast of Dunbar Wharf I began to think of the Duncan Dunbars, that remarkable father and son, who had been responsible for so much of the nautical prosperity in this neighbourhood during the early part of the nineteenth century.

The father had arrived in Limehouse from his native home in Scotland, bringing little else with him but an industrious nature and a reputation for being a hard-headed business man. Before long he had become a successful wine and spirit merchant and an exporter of the local ale brewed in Fore Street, which was the previous name given to the eastern end of Narrow Street. But his greatest triumph was when he became the proud owner of his first fine sailing-ship. By the end of his life Duncan Dunbar was a ship-owner of no mean standing, and because of the flourishing trade he had established with India and the Far East, many of his vessels were built in Burma of the finest local teak. About this time the bottled beer from the Limehouse Brewery was christened "India Pale Ale".

Duncan Dunbar's eldest son became a partner in his father's firm two years before the old man died. He inherited a small commercial empire and his maritime enterprises were so successful that a rabbit-warren of ship's stores, sail-lofts, warehouses and tally-clerks offices grew up on both sides of Limekiln Creek, to supply his fleet of splendid sailing-vessels when they returned from their long voyages.

Between 1830 and 1840 the whole district had become a swarming beehive of nautical activities. But it was not until the discovery of gold in Australia in 1851, that Duncan Dunbar's empire reached its peak. The shrewd Scottish ship-owner hastily ordered a number of large passenger-ships to be built, with which to transport some of the thousands who were anxious to profit from the Australian gold rush. At the same time he made the lucrative discovery that India Ale suited the palates of the emigrants to such a remarkable degree that his ships never set sail without a substantial cargo of that thirst-quenching beverage in their holds.

This distinguished ship-owner suddenly dropped dead

Dunbar's Wharf, a few doors from us, in Narrow Street.

at the age of fifty-eight, leaving property to the value of a million and a half sterling.

The warehouses bearing the name of Duncan Dunbar are still in use today, and it does not take a big stretch of the imagination to picture Narrow Street in those halcyon years of the 19th century; the whole place a maze of sail-maker's lofts, rope stores and mast-maker's yards, and the air filled with the pungent smell of Stockholm tar, oakum and fresh timber from the forests of Northern Europe. It was a common sight to see the bowsprit and figurehead of some barque or schooner under repair projecting over half the roadway, or the tall masts of a China tea clipper arising majestically above the roof-tops until they seemed to touch the very stars in the sky.

I continued happily daydreaming until a monstrous lorry, travelling at headlong speed towards Aberdeen Wharf, missed me by a hair's-breadth, whereupon I returned with a sudden jolt to the 20th century and crossed the road into the less precarious backwater of Three Colts Street. The dog pulled ahead optimistically as she suspected that we were heading for the churchyard, a small green oasis amidst the wilderness of bricks and mortar.

Half way along Three Colts Street I noticed an oldish man standing outside a café known as Doll's Den. He was very thin and his shoulders were bent under the weight of a sackful of logs, but he appeared to be bubbling over with suppressed excitement. As I approached he began to run his fingers through the wiry black fur on Texel's back. "That's a lovely dawg you got there," he remarked conversationally. "Do 'e bite?"

"Only women, as a rule," I replied, hoping that she

would not decide to make an exception to the rule on this occasion.

"Dawgs is better than 'umans ter my mind," observed the old man. "They don't give no trouble an' you can always rely on 'em."

We all padded along the street in a companionable silence for a few minutes, after which our escort suddenly confided to me that he was an old-age pensioner and his name was Mr Kitt. "Same as Eartha Kitt, only not quite the same, see what I mean?" he added, with a throaty chuckle.

I saw what he meant quite clearly, and we parted at the entrance to the churchyard in a most amicable manner.

Owing to the balmy autumn weather the wooden benches lining the pathway on the north side of the church were in full occupation. There was a hairy old tramp clutching a newspaper package on the first one, who eyed the dog malevolently and mumbled something which sounded like: "Grrr! Fuck off," when she started sniffing at his coat. A few yards farther along the path sat a pair of oldish women wearing beige felt hats and shapeless tweed coats, who were discussing their latest medical symptoms with obvious relish. On the third bench reclined a solitary Chinaman, contemplating the gold and yellow carpet of fallen leaves around him with a remote and inscrutable glimmer of a smile hovering near the corners of his mouth. And the last bench of all was occupied by a pair of lean and handsome youths from Jack's Palace, who were deeply engrossed in a book called "Nicholl's Seamanship and Nautical Knowledge". I overheard one of them say to the other; "I bet you'll never get your mate's ticket if they ask you this one, Jock! Just you listen... A derrick 40 feet long has to lift a weight of 6 tons with a guntackle purchase; the span is made fast 50 feet above the keel and the purchase fall is led down the derrick. Find the stress on the span and the thrust on the derrick, assuming the weight plumbs a point 25 feet from the mast?"

Texel and I emerged from the churchyard by a small gate on the northern boundary, and crossed Commercial Road to the corner of Salmon Lane. There was a group of West Indians lounging on the steps of the seamen's hostel, known to most sailors as the Stack of Bricks; and farther along the road women with bulging shopping-baskets were hurrying to and fro. There was an air of bustling activity about the shopping precincts; a sort of cheerful Friday morning feeling which seemed to hint that it was pay-day today and the week-end was at hand, and there would be tripe and onions or eels and mash washed down with a few pints of Guinness; and, taking all things into consideration, it wasn't such a bad old world after all!

Behind the counter in Bartons, the bakery, Miss Higgins was putting the finishing touches to a pink and white confection adorned with forty-three multi-coloured candles, which bore the legend "Happy Birthday Mum". All around her a brisk interchange of local gossip, loaves of bread, jam tarts and doughnuts, and sharp repartee was taking place. I had just bought some salmon and cucumber sandwiches and a hot sausage roll, when a gruff female voice behind me remarked inquisitively; "I see'd you 'ad some visitors on your roof early this mornin', but I knew there wasn't nuffink te worry abaht wiv the ole dawg there te pertect youse."

I assumed a serious expression and refrained from

disillusioning the old woman about our dog, at the same time thinking to myself that there were extraordinarily few happenings, no matter what hour of the day or night they occurred, which passed unnoticed in our neighbourhood. Meanwhile a small but select social gathering seemed to be lingering for longer than usual in Barton's Bakery, intent on hearing a first hand recital of our adventures at daybreak. Once I had given it to them, their united reaction was quite definite: "Fucking coppers! Orways pokin' their noses into uvver people's business. Pity your 'ubby didn't frow 'em orff the roof!"

I was a bit startled by this blood-thirsty attitude as I have always regarded the London policeman as a strong courageous defender of the weak and persecuted, a sort of father figure who exudes a soothing atmosphere of peace and security wherever he goes.

A few minutes later I crossed Salmon Lane to buy some groceries and noticed old Pop trotting happily along the pavement with a leg of lamb peeping out of his shopping-bag. Although he turned ninety more than a year ago, he always looks more spruce and debonair than most men half his age. His daughter once told us that her father only weighed 3 lbs when he was born, and as there were no incubators in Limehouse then, he was reared inside a bale of hay in front of the fire. Seeing Pop go by nearly a century later, one feels that there must be some undetected moral to this story.

Outside the V.G. Stores the fishmonger, Albert, had set up his Friday morning stall and a long queue of housewives were waiting to be served. His fingers worked deftly and swiftly, filleting, cleaning and wrapping up portions of haddock, plaice, rock salmon, eel, cod and fresh farm eggs in last week's East London Advertiser; and whilst he worked he carried on a lively and highly topical monologue, never drawing breath for one second. It sounded something like this –

"'Ello, darlin'! 'Ow's yer ole man treatin' you? I gotta nice bit o' fresh 'addock fer youse today. If things is that bad I'd git the law on te 'im. Poor ole cow! Bin up the 'orspital yet? Whatcher, Maisie! Two pahnd o' rock salmon did you say? Orright, darlin'! No good bawlin' at 'im like that; poor li'l sod. Did you 'ear that young Ernie bin locked up? Best boy that ever drew breff, I reckon 'e was. A nice big juicy eel is what you want, Muvver. Come straight arta the North Sea specially fer youse lot! Don't nevver say young Albert don't look arta yer interests ...."

The two fruit and vegetable stalls were also doing a brisk trade, and on the other side of the road a smart claret-coloured limousine had just drawn up outside the Good Friends Restaurant, its occupants gazing rather nervously at the animated scene. Good Friends belonged to a famous Chinese restaurateur called Charlie Chang who, some years ago, owned a chain of "Friendly" eating places all over Chinatown. There was New Friends, Old Friends, Local Friends and City Friends; but the most celebrated one of all is Good Friends in Salmon Lane, which preserves its oriental dignity behind a narrow rafia-curtained door attached to which is a small cardboard notice firmly stating, "Reservations Only".

I retraced my steps along Salmon Lane, heavily laden with the week-end shopping. The church steeple was soaring amongst a bank of cumulus at the far end of the street, and back in the churchyard a gentle sun was shining compassionately through the red and golden glory of the autumn foliage upon the flotsam and jetsam of East London. Every so often an old tramp would look up from his silent reverie and raise a knarled hand to shield his eyes from the radiant scene around him. And a few yards away in Commercial Road the lorries and cars roared by, oblivious to everything except the speed of their progress across the great metropolis.

I always brought Texel's yellow ball with me on these expeditions, as she loved to run after it and retrieve it from the long grass. She had been given, and lost, many balls during her lifetime, but this particular one had a charmed life for it had outlasted any of its predecessors and she seemed to regard it with a special affection. That morning I threw the ball with all my strength and it disappeared amongst some bushes bordering the east side of the churchyard, but the dog made off in exactly the opposite direction as she had picked up the scent of another animal approaching through the western entrance. After a great deal of whistling, stamping of feet and general irritation, I managed to catch Texel and take her round to the other side of the church to hunt for her ball; but it was nowhere to be found. We searched under every bush and fallen leaf, in all the gullies and nooks and crannies, but it had apparently been spirited away into some invisible aperture. After half an hour or so we abandoned the search and left the churchyard in low spirits. The dog felt guilty and upset because she had not followed the ball in the first place, and I was angry with her for losing her most special plaything.

In this exasperated frame of mind we took a short cut

through the Barley Mow Estate, where the new thirteen storey miniature skyscrapers had recently been completed. It was not long before I became aware of a woman converging on our course, who was also plodding along in a lop-sided manner under the weight of a heavy shopping-bag. Although I had never seen her before to the best of my knowledge, she appeared to have something on her mind which she wished to impart to me at the earliest possible opportunity.

"Ello, darlin!" she called out, as soon as I was within hailing distance. "1 seed you bin shoppin' up Salmons Lane same as me, but I betcher'll never guess what 'appened te me jus' when I was crossin' over the main road?"

I admitted that I had no idea, for she didn't look as though she'd been run down by a lorry although, on closer inspection, she did seem to be clutching her right hip in a curious manner.

"Well, darlin', I'd jus' stepped orff the pavement when the eelastic in me drawers gives way!" she confided to me explosively. There was a pause whilst she waited for this information to sink in and have its due effect, then she continued cheerfully: "Them drawers they sells you up the Co-op ain't fit te clean the winders wiv. I sez te my Doris only las' week I sez, I betcher that eelastic'll let me dahn one o' these fine days, and now look what's 'appened. I'm goin' back there temorrer te sort aht the manager, see if I don't!"

On that warlike note we parted, and a few minutes later Texel and I reached home.

I had just dragged the shopping up our steep staircase to the kitchen on the second floor, when the front door bell rang. I cursed noisily and ran back down the stairs to open the door. And lo and behold, there was Mr Kitt standing on the pavement holding out Texel's yellow ball, with his eyes screwed up into little slits as if he was enjoying some rather special private joke. I was filled with astonishment as I began to pelt him with questions as to how he knew she'd lost the ball, where he'd found it and how he'd discovered where we lived.

"I seed you 'untin' fer it when I come back dahn Three Colts Street," he replied; "so I goes in arta you'd gorn an finds it tucked up under a yeller leaf, a yeller one mark you, by the corner o' the church. 'E won't 'alf be pleased te git is ball back, I sez te myself, so I 'urries straight rahnd 'ere. That's

my place up the top there," he continued, pointing to a window in the top right hand corner of Brightlingsea Buildings; "an' I'se watched you an' the ole dawg go in an' aht o' this door almos' every day!"

A small cloud which had been drifting across the face of the sun reached the far side at that identical moment, and suddenly all the minor irritations of the morning disappeared in the sheer pleasure of being alive in Narrow Street on a fine Friday morning.

Mr Kitt, who lived across the road in Brightlingsea Buildings.

Chapter V

The Barge Yard

"I've got a small parcel for you locked up in my office," George announced importantly. "And I've took special care of it on account of the label marked FRAGILE on the outside."

Dick and I were standing on the pavement outside the barge-yard when George, the foreman, had noticed us there and beckoned to us to come inside. We thanked him warmly for taking in our parcels whenever the postman called and we were out, and he replied that it was no bother to him at all but, as far as he was concerned, Narrow Street ended at Number 88, going in a westerly direction so to speak, and the rest of it could fend for itself! We felt honoured to be included just inside George's boundary, especially after he had elaborated on the reasons for this demarcation line which were not particularly flattering to some of our immediate neighbours.

George was in his early sixties when we had first made his acquaintance after our arrival in Narrow Street. He was a tall man with a strong weather-beaten face, and he wore dark-rimmed spectacles through which a pair of very shrewd blue eyes kept a close watch on what was going on around him.

George had been born and bred on the Marsh, and he was extremely proud of this fact. The Marsh is the U-shaped bulge of land on the south side of the river, terminating in Blackwall Point, which the ignorant are apt to refer to as East Greenwich and which has now shed most of its native population in order to make room for the wide motorway

The Limehouse waterfront in the early years of the 20th Century; our house is behind the inner barge sails.

leading down into the Blackwall Tunnel. The Marsh dwellers were a small seafaring community who did not mix readily with the hoi polloi from other parts of London. For the most part they were educated at the Dreadnought School, an imposing Victorian pile which dominates the network of small streets around the South Metropolitan Gas Works, and they seldom chose their partners in marriage from anywhere beyond the frontier formed by the Trafalgar Road. Even less would they have contemplated an alliance with a foreigner from the north bank of the river. George was no exception to the rule and his wife, who had also been reared on the Marsh, shared his sentiments about its supreme desirability as a place to live in.

When he was a young man George had learnt his trade as a shipwright under the guidance of Mr Norton, a famous Greenwich barge builder from whose slipway many a fine Thames sailing-barge was launched into the muddy waters of Bugsby's Reach. By the time he had finished his apprenticeship there was very little he did not know about the ancient art of barge building, and combined with this knowledge, George had developed a certain commanding presence and downright honesty about his whole demeanour which could not fail to impress all who knew him. He was a Triton amongst the minnows, as the old saying goes, and although he ruled the barge yard with an almost naval discipline, there was never a day when a cheerful symphony of hammering, sawing, singing, welding and laughter did not emanate from that three hundred-year-old crazy wooden structure, poised so precariously on the edge of the river.

Besides George there was Ron, who had also worked on the river all his life, and Jim with the infinitely deep voice, who sang old-time music-hall songs in the holds of barges in which he was working; then there was Bill and Duggie and old Joe, the engineer, who used to turn up in a different car every other day because 'the wife wasn't easy to please'. And

Jim, Ron and Bill celebrating the launching of our new dinghy with Dick.

finally, David, who had long brown hair and liquid brown eyes which were not slow to appreciate the au pair girls sunbathing in bikinis on the balcony of Number 86. One day I found old Joe standing on the pavement outside the barge yard glaring ferociously at a man on the other side of the road. He drew me aside, without averting his gaze for one second, and whispered ominously in my left ear: "There's a stranger loiterin' about over by the Black Horse; but I won't let 'im out of my sight so don't you worry girl. If there's any trouble round here I'll soon get hold of a copper."

I had always imagined before that London was the one place where a stranger might pass through the streets unobserved, but once again it was forcibly brought home to me that nothing ever passed unobserved round our way.

Amongst the barges outside our house there was an old veteran called "Marraine" which had not been used for a good many years, and she was a particular favourite of ours on account of the flowers which grew in her hold. I liked to imagine that some idealistic seagull had dropped the seeds 'en passant', with a little earth to encourage them to feel at home; and then one spring a brilliant medley of daisies, dandelions and rose-bay willow-herbs appeared in the middle of that rusty iron hull, a secret floating garden only visible to the birds and those who lived just above the barge.

One fine morning I was busy at my typewriter beside the window in Trevor's pad. I had been alternately typing and gazing affectionately at "Marraine" for several hours, when suddenly I noticed Duggie squatting on the bluff bows of the barge only a few yards away from the window, imitating me using my typewriter. He had poised a five gallon petrol can on the gunwale in front of him, and with many extravagant gestures of the arms and eyebrows he gave a vivid demonstration of how I appeared to him, as seen from the river. His performance was so comical that I nearly choked, and it became increasingly difficult to concentrate on my work. However, it was not long before another diversion caused us both to think of other things.

It was a singularly peaceful morning with soft fluffy clouds drifting across a pale blue sky and hardly a ripple to disturb the shining surface of the river which lay drowsing in the midday heat. But suddenly the still atmosphere was rent by a deep, gruff voice which sounded far from peaceful:

"Duggie" roared Mrs Dorothea Woodward Fisher, O.B.E.; "Duggie, why aren't you chipping?"

Duggie, whose lungs were considerably less powerful than those of his employer, mumbled a semi-audible excuse and hastily produced some tools from his dungaree pockets with which he started repairing some trifling imperfection on the foredeck of "Marraine".

I craned my neck out of the window and saw a small oldish lady standing on the catwalk outside the barge yard, pinching George's right ear-lobe between her forefinger and thumb whilst she bellowed at him in a persuasive manner: "Those three tugs I sent you last evening, my boy; I want them ready for work by Friday dinner-time!"

George drew himself up to his full height and assumed a severe expression, while he detailed for her six good reasons why her request could not be complied with; but they both of them knew, without a shadow of doubt, that those tugs would be ready by Friday dinner-time.

Mrs Woodward Fisher, who was seventy-six at that time, was wearing an Edwardian masculine-styled tailor trimmed

Mrs Woodward-Fisher on one of her tugs.

with a velvet collar and cuffs, and a soft shirt beneath the jacket which was held together at the throat by a dashing blue and white spotted cravat, and at the wrists by large square-cut cufflinks. Her hair was arranged in a crisp and wind-resistant manner, and she wore a gold-rimmed monocle in her left eye. A glint of gold was also visible amongst her teeth when she turned to roar at Duggie again, and more than a glint on her fingers which were covered in heavy old-fashioned rings and gripped a long tortoise-shell cigarette-holder from which she emitted a decisive puff of smoke at regular intervals. Many people who met Mrs Woodward Fisher for the first time imagined that she was an artist or an actress; one even suggested that she might be a butterfly collector! But it seldom occurred to them that she was one of the most astute barge and tug owners on the River Thames, who could handle the toughest tug-boat skipper or the most turbulent meeting of the Dock Labour Board with equal impunity. She was often known as Mother Thames or the Uncrowned Queen of the Thames.

Mrs Woodward Fisher was always in trouble as a child, so her family sent her to Cheltenham Ladies' College with a view to turning her into a refined and ladylike young woman. Even in those days she was possessed of a remarkable intelligence and a nimble wit, and her youthful ambition was to become a barrister.

She ran away from home at the age of seventeen and went to live with her grandmother. During that period she was taken to a dance one night, and there she met a Thames lighterman called Billy Woodward Fisher who was a beautiful dancer. He completely swept her off her feet with the result that she abandoned the highly eligible young man to whom she was engaged at the time, and turned her whole life towards the River Thames. Dorothea married her lighterman during the first World War, and they lived happily together for the next forty-eight years.

Billy Woodward Fisher was born on the Isle of Dogs in 1889. He was a fine athlete in his youth, winning many prizes for boxing, running and, most of all, for sculling. In 1911 he became the first boy from Millwall to win the famous Doggett's Coat and Badge Race and he achieved this victory in the fastest time it has ever been rowed, either before or since.

The young Woodward Fishers started their married life in a flat in Waller Road, New Cross, for which they paid approximately 43p a week. A few years later, when Dorothea was twenty-three, they bought their first barge for £20. It was the year 1918.

"He was the practical one and I had the business brain," Mrs Woodward Fisher recalls nostalgically. "If I'd had a sweet girlish voice I wouldn't have got anywhere, would I?"

Over the years that remarkable couple built up a fleet of eighty-eight barges and twelve tugs which collected cargoes of grain, timber, corned beef, grapefruit and cables from the large freighters which used the Surrey Commercial Docks, and distributed them up and down the banks of the Thames and Medway, anywhere between Reading and Maidstone, and all over the canal network in the London area as well. They also acquired the old barge builder's yard and moorings in Limehouse, a wharf in Millwall and a massive Victorian house in Lewisham.

Mrs Woodward Fisher gave birth to a son and a daughter, and in addition to bringing up the children she

Mrs Woodward-Fisher at home with her parrot.

organized the clerical side of the business, and could often be found working alongside her husband pumping out barges to keep them afloat.

"Mother is undoubtedly the boss," Mr Woodward Fisher often remarked, "She's a marvel the way she organizes. It's not always easy to deal with men on the river, but Mother does it wonderfully. She handles the Unions too. There's not a man on the river who knows more about barges than my wife. She does a lot in the garden too, for she's very keen on roses."

Mr Woodward Fisher was always known to his own family as "The Guv'nor" and to most other people as Bill.

During the Second World War many of the Guv'nor's barges played a small but valiant part in the invasion of Europe. They were converted into motor-barges, powered by twin 100 H.P. Chrysler engines, and they crossed to

Shore barges fixing their towing-rope as they approach the sailing barges, ordinary barges, tugs and cargo ships on the Thames.

Normandy on D-Day with the great invasion fleet. The crews of those squat and homely-looking vessels toiled day and night at Arromanches, Port-en-Bessin and Caen, where the docks had all been destroyed and cargo ships could not enter the harbour. They landed countless tons of vital ammunition, food and medical supplies all along the Continental coastline, and helped to bring succour to the starving Dutch at the end of the war.

During the summer of 1945 the first convoy of twenty-five power-barge-ramps, as they were called in those days, came back from Terneuzen. Many of them were covered in battle scars and had the names Arromanches, Caen, Ostende, Ghent, Rotterdam, Nijmegen and the Rhine Crossing proudly painted along their sides. They sailed all night and when one of them sprang a leak in the middle of the North Sea, she was lashed between two of her sister barges and the cumbersome trio struggled on across the heaving waters. The tug "Hero" came down to Tilbury to meet them and escort them upriver to Quebec Dock where they were given a real hero's welcome home.

Of the twenty Woodward Fisher barges, all named after fish, which went to war, only three of them came home again. Even to this day I can see "Lancing", one of the three, floating peacefully amongst the covey of barges just below our windows. Her working days are over now, but she still serves as a mooring barge to which her more transitory sisters can secure themselves when they come to be repaired at the old barge yard.

Billy Woodward Fisher died suddenly in 1964, and his ashes were scattered on the waters of the Thames in Limehouse Reach. His dearest wish had always been to build a fine clubhouse for the Poplar, Blackwall and District Rowing Club on the shores of the Isle of Dogs; and on that tragic May morning when all his friends had collected in Limehouse to mourn his passing, Mrs Woodward Fisher made a vow that this wish should be fulfilled. After all, the Guv'nor had been a member of the club for fifty-six years and its president for the past twenty-five years, so that the struggle to achieve this ambition was something which appealed to the valiant spirit of his widow.

Several years later Dick and I drove across to Lewisham one evening to visit Mother Thames on a matter of business. We were astonished to find a small mountain of jumble in the middle of the drive leading to her front door; old furniture, crockery, books, pictures and odds and ends jostled each other for supremacy of position, and just behind them was parked Mrs Woodward Fisher's white Jaguar. We learnt afterwards that she and her sister managed to raise nearly a £1,000 a year for the Grove Park Hospital by means of this amazing hotchpotch of unwanted articles. After some careful circumnavigation we succeeded in reaching the front door which was opened for us by Mrs Woodward Fisher's sister, accompanied by a vast Weimaraner dog called Max and nine cats. She invited us to step inside and it was like entering a museum of maritime memories. All around us were ship's bells, steering-wheels, tropical fish in tanks that were lit up from inside, plaques of ancient sailing-ships, china figures of sailors and many old pictures and prints of nautical scenes on the River Thames. Perhaps the most prized possession of all was the Guv'nor's scarlet Doggett coat and silver badge which he had won in 1911.

Mrs Woodward Fisher was waiting for us at the top of a narrow staircase with a rope bannister, which reminded me of a ship's companionway. She was wearing one of her severely-cut Edwardian tailors with a tartan waistcoat under the jacket and a festive Paisley bow-tie at the neck, and she had a parrot called Laura perched on her right shoulder.

We were ushered into a small apartment which she informed us, with a certain pride, was her radio-room. It soon transpired that it was the heart of the Woodward Fisher empire, from which Mother Thames directed and controlled all her tugs, barges and miscellaneous nautical enterprises up and down the river. Her desk was festooned with telephones and radio operator's equipment, and from the roof of her house a cluster of radio aerials swayed dizzily above the chimney-pots of Lewisham, like a field of summer corn undulating in the wind.

Mrs Woodward Fisher offered Dick a cigar from a mammoth box in the top drawer of her desk, and told us that they had been sent to her by a grateful skipper who always addressed her as "Old Cock" on the telephone.

"I've had a marvellous life," she told us. "But it breaks my heart to see the river as it is today. The derelict look of the big warehouses, good strong barges lying around idle and crying out for a lick of paint..... I can remember the days when the docks were packed with beautiful barges; and one lighterman for every six boats."

We asked her what she thought was the reason for this dwindling of trade in what was once the greatest port in the world. She thought for a few seconds before replying rather sadly: "It's hard to pin it down to any one thing. The growth of road transport; lorries can shift cargo much quicker and cheaper. Lack of enterprise; lazy men, but bad masters too; crushing restrictions and Trade Union disputes which have undermined barge traffic and priced it out of the market. Most of the problems are due to the fact that no one is willing to work a forty-eight hour week nowadays."

She took a long pull at her cigar, settled the parrot on her right shoulder and continued; "Oh, they'll come to their senses eventually. Owners, unions, all of 'em. They'll have to, darling. I believe that the River Thames is like an old apple tree during a hard winter, but come the springtime the little apples will grow again; perhaps not as big and red and juicy as they once were, but they'll grow alright. But my goodness me, I wish they'd get a move on!"

She puffed angrily at her cigar for a few seconds, then, quite suddenly, her whole face lit up like a shaft of sunlight bursting through the storm-clouds, and she exclaimed excitedly: "I want you two to come to the opening of our new boat-house on the Isle of Dogs on September 26th. Put it down in your diary now so that you won't forget the date!"

As we left the radio room Mrs Woodward Fisher called down the companionway after us: "Have a look at the jumble in the drive on your way out, darlings. You might see something you'd like to buy there."

On the morning of September 26th, 1970, the sun was shining brilliantly out of a cloudless sapphire-blue sky, and the river danced and sparkled in tones of blue, green, silver and gold and looked as if it might burst into song at the slightest provocation.

Across the water the three tall masts of the "Cutty Sark"

rose triumphantly above the roofs and chimney-pots of Greenwich, and the Royal Naval College lay smiling in the sunlight, secure in the knowledge of its own incomparable beauty. Dick and I were drinking champagne on the terrace of the Poplar, Blackwall and District Rowing-Club's new boat-house, and amongst the cheerful milling throng around us there was an impression of intense excitement and exhilaration in the air.

It was a momentous day in the life of Mrs Woodward Fisher; a magnificent ideal and the Guvnor's last wish, for which she had striven with all her might for the past sixteen years, had at last been fulfilled. It had taken her ten years to extract a strip of land on a sixty year lease from the G.L.C., and a further six years to achieve the comparatively minor target of collecting £70,000 to build her boat-house! The result was certainly something to be proud of, for one of the finest boat-houses in the country had arisen, as if by magic, on the site of the old North Greenwich Railway Station alongside Scrap Iron Park on the Isle of Dogs.

In the old days the members of the rowing-club were mainly watermen, dockers, stevedores, lightermen and boiler-makers from the ship repair yards on the island, but nowadays there are also a few bank clerks, builders, accountants, policemen and a handsome young man from the Foreign Office called John Doble. I shall never forget the day he first turned up in Limehouse, just after we had moved into Number 88.

I was busy scrubbing the kitchen floor one morning when I heard the bell ring, so I ran downstairs to open the door; and there was a tall princely stranger standing on the door-step asking if I knew of anyone who had a bed-sitter to let in Narrow Street. I noticed his anxious eyes probing the inner recesses of our hall in the hope of spotting the object of his quest somewhere down at the river end of the ground floor, so I hastened to tell him that we had only one bedroom in our house but it might be worth his while asking at Number 80, as they sometimes had a flat to let.

He went away and I returned to my work, but half an hour later he was back again looking more disconsolate than ever. He said that he had tried every house in Narrow Street without success; then he went on to tell me that he was in the Foreign Office and had just returned from a few years abroad, and as he was now due for a spell in London he wanted to find somewhere to live. I pointed out that somewhere around St. James's or Westminster might be more appropriate and closer to his office, whereupon he explained to me in a long-suffering voice, as one might talk to a rather dense and backward child, that in his opinion Limehouse was the only possible place in London in which to settle with any degree of happiness. Suddenly he struck me as being remarkably intelligent, for he was voicing our own special feelings about the place which were not shared by all our acquaintances. So I asked him in and gave him Mrs Woodward Fisher's telephone number, thinking that she might be able to help him.

We heard nothing further until about eighteen months later, when Dick and I came home one evening to find a small yellow car, with the curved post-horns of the German Postal Service painted on its sides, parked outside Number 96. We were bending over it trying to guess what it was doing in the middle of Limehouse when the owner suddenly loomed up behind us, and it turned out to be none other than John Doble.

He told us that he had just moved into the "Rabbit-hutch", as Number 96 is always called, having at last persuaded Mrs Woodward Fisher to rent it to him; and this minute flat seemed to him like a small corner of heaven.

Not long afterwards we noticed a varnished dinghy called "Lily of Limehouse" moored to the wooden piles supporting the house next to ours; and for many months to follow, on a fine morning when the tide was hurrying upriver towards the City and Westminster, it was possible to catch a glimpse of the young diplomat, clad in a smart Savile Row suit, setting off to work in his dinghy.

Despite the difference of half a century in their ages, there was a certain similarity of outlook between John and his landlady. They both belonged to the "Never Say Die" brigade and they seldom lost the courage of their convictions. They seemed to be inspired by the same sort of dogged determination in the pursuit of some worthwhile aim; and they shared the same love of boats and maritime adventures.

John Doble and his little German post car outside his home in the Rabbit-hutch.

Limehouse Lil with John Doble's new house in Narrow Street below it.

At seventy-seven Mrs Woodward Fisher had enough energy left to wear out the strongest bargee, and although she often became deeply depressed by the problems of her beloved river, she had no intention of sinking without a good few splashes. The names of some of her tugs, "Ikangoit", "Ikanopit", "Shalldo", "Willdo" and "Kando", were all selected to hit back at the Port of London Authority and the National Dock Labour Board.

"God's going to help," she declared with firm conviction; and every evening she went to church to make sure. He didn't forget about Woodward Fisher's nautical enterprises.

One evening a big freighter of Ellerman's Wilson Line steamed along Limehouse Reach about the time of high water. Her wash spread outwards in ever-widening circles, a mighty upheaval of the sleeping black river. Beneath our windows Mother Thames's barges, those squat iron monsters with all the fishy names like "Hake", "Stickleback", "Minnow", "Dab", "Limpet", "Sardine" and "Surgeon-fish", clanged together with a low-pitched thunderous uproar, a brave defiant sort of noise which would never admit the word DEFEAT.

Chapter VI

The Grapes

There are no soft undulations or vague contours in the Limehouse silhouette. It is a region of bold strong outlines; of tall cranes, mighty chimneys, dark warehouses and immense blocks of Council flats which stand out in stark relief against the evening sky.

At the close of a fine autumn day when the sun begins to sink behind Tower Bridge into a bed of gold and purple clouds, reflecting some of its departing glory in a thousand windows all over East London, an observant wanderer on the Rotherhithe shore might notice a rosy glow filtering through a bow-fronted window suspended above the dark river on the north bank, just beneath the dominant shape of Limehouse Lil; and he might even receive a cheerful impression of good company enjoying warm and pleasant surroundings inside that window, sending down shafts of radiance on to the dark and muddy foreshore below.

For more than three hundred years a small public-house has stood on that curve of the river in Limehouse Reach, only a few cables away from the entrance to Limehouse Cut on the one side and Limehouse Hole on the other. The slender wooden piles which support the back of the house resemble a trio of spindly old legs clad in mottled green and brown stockings, and they have become so firmly established in the glutinous black mud that they are quite impervious to the ebb and flow of the restless tides. There is a small jetty where the colliers tie up, only a stone's throw from the balcony; and downriver from there lie Mrs

The Grapes public house in olden days.

Winkle on a barge in front of The Grapes, and two customers on the balcony behind her.

Woodward Fisher's barge moorings.

As long ago as 1820, when Charles Dickens used to visit his godfather in Limehouse, The Grapes was thought of as a very old tavern, and as a child Dickens was known to have sung there while standing on the tables. In his novel "Our Mutual Friend" he gives a vivid description of the place which he calls the Six Jolly Fellowship-Porters, from which it might easily be recognised to this very day: "The Six Jolly Fellowship-Porters, already mentioned as a tavern of a dropsical appearance, had long settled down into a state of hale infirmity. In its whole constitution it had not a straight floor, and hardly a straight line; but it had outlasted, and clearly would outlast, many a better-trimmed building, many a sprucer public-house. Externally, it was a narrow lop-sided jumble of corpulent windows heaped one upon another as you might heap as many toppling oranges, with a crazy wooden verandah impending over the water; indeed the whole house, inclusive of the complaining flag-staff on the roof, impended over the water, but seemed to have got into the condition of a faint-hearted diver who has paused so long on the brink that he will never go in at all.

"This description applies to the river frontage of the Six Jolly Fellowship-Porters. The back of the establishment, though the chief entrance was there, so contracted, that it merely represented in its connexion with the front, the handle of a flat-iron set upright on its broadest end. This handle stood at the bottom of a wilderness of courts and alleys; which wilderness pressed so hard and close upon the Six Jolly Fellowship-Porters as to leave the hostelry not an inch of ground beyond its door. For this reason, in combination with the fact that

Renie and Jack on the balcony of The Grapes.

Narrow Street in later years, with Booty's at one end, our house the blue one in the middle, and The Grapes at the far end.

the house was all but afloat at high water, when the Porters had a family wash the linen subjected to that operation might usually be seen drying on lines stretched across the reception-rooms and bedchambers."

Nowadays there is no array of wet linen fluttering above the heads of the customers in the saloon or public bars, and the wilderness of courts and alleys does not press so hard and close upon the front door; but in other respects the place has changed but little, and when Dickens tells us in a later paragraph that the bar of the Six Jolly Fellowship-Porters was a bar to soften the human breast, and the available space in it was not much larger than a hackney-coach, anyone who knows the place well would be inclined to agree with him whole-heartedly.

Over the years The Grapes has remained a typical small Limehouse pub, retaining much of its ancient seafaring flavour and attracting a steady local trade combined with a few adventurous visitors from other parts of the world, The reason that it has survived the fate of many riverside pubs and is still very much the same as it was when Dickens knew it, was due to the landlord, Jack Phillips, who resisted all temptations to make it into a celebrated tourist attraction and a huge commercial success.

Jack and his wife, Renie, were both born and bred in Limehouse. He came of a seafaring family and grew up in Number 86, the house next to ours. He was a Freeman of the River and worked for many years on Thames sailing-barges before he decided to become a publican. Renie came from Brightlingsea Buildings just across the road, and her grandfather was a sail-maker during the great days of the East and West India Docks, when they were filled with barques and schooners, the tall masts of which rose above the warehouses and dock walls to mingle with the stars. Even her grandmother was in close touch with the sea, for she made the flags which many of those ships flew so proudly from their spars. So it is hardly surprising that the maritime traditions of that bygone age should still be fostered and kept alive in the cosy and hospitable interior of The Grapes.

Dick and me, with The Grapes on the left.

Jack Phillips, when occasion demanded, could be as stubborn and inflexible as an iron bar and as uncommunicative as a deaf-mute. He was not one of your garrulous landlords, spreading the gossip of the neighbourhood with a glib tongue and an easy manner. On the contrary, he was much more inclined to look you over with a certain air of reserved appraisal, until he had taken your measure and decided whether or not you were fit company for the long-established fraternity of the public bar. But those he knew and trusted saw the gentler side of his character. A smile of exceptional sweetness illuminated his face as he greeted some old acquaintance, and he had an inimitable way of pouring out the right drink for each of his regular customers before they even approached within asking distance of the bar.

Renie, his wife, had a toughness of character which carried her smiling through the worst ordeals. She suffered from few illusions about her customers, and if anyone chanced to provoke an unpleasant atmosphere by their bad behaviour or undesirable remarks, Renie was the one who withered them with a few choice epithets and quickly dispatched them through that narrow entrance, back to the gloomy night outside.

She was like a queen in her own bar; and she always appeared impeccably turned out, as if for some special occasion, with her blonde hair carefully waved and an inexhaustable fund of interesting titbits and sharp repartee with which to entertain her clientele.

The public bar in The Grapes is a long narrow room with the bar occupying some two thirds of the left-hand side. The door from Narrow Street leads straight into it, and this is the only way of entering the pub except by a steep iron ladder which connects the balcony with the foreshore at low water. There are a few wooden benches and tables set against the walls, but for the most part the fraternity of the public bar prefer to stand so that they can circulate more easily amongst their friends, emphasize the highlights of some anecdote with sweeping motions of the arms, and generally enjoy the freedom of expression which is denied to those who sit huddled over their drinks in some obscure corner.

Amongst the regulars you are sure to find a handful of men from the Stepney Power Station; a few seamen from one of the colliers which bring coal for Limehouse Lil from Newcastle or South Wales; a lorry-driver or two on their way home to the eastern suburbs; the Reverend Charles Watts, rector of St. Anne's Church; Jimmy Jones, a big-hearted Yorkshireman; one or two couples from Brightlingsea Buildings or Faraday Dwellings across the road; and, last but not least, old Pop, Renie's father.

Dick and I were leaning on the bar one evening listening to Billy Taxi, a lorry-driver from Chingford, who had a special anecdote that he wished to impart to all those within earshot. He took a long pull at his tankard, cleared his throat experimentally, then launched into a vivid account of how he was setting off on his holiday to Majorca when who should he notice sitting in the very next seat to him on the aeroplane but Mr Watts! As soon as the plane had taken off and risen above the clouds, an air-hostess came round with a tray of bottles and glasses, so he promptly invited the rector to join him in a drop of the hard stuff; but, much to his surprise, Mr Watts shook his head emphatically and replied: "No, thank you very much,

Billy. I won't have one just now; too near Head Office see?"

Mr Watts, who had heard the story before, pretended to be deeply engrossed in a theological discussion with a C.I.D. inspector, and farther along the bar an immense docker called Neddy, who can sing like an angel, was just beginning to give a full-blooded rendering of "Daisy Bell". For a few seconds all conversation ceased as waves of pure music drifted up to the ceiling then hovered in joyful clusters of crotchets and quavers above the layer of smoke which had gathered in a thin grey mantle over the heads of the drinkers. Half a dozen powerful male voices joined in the chorus, and a pint tankard banged emphatically on the bar in the adjoining room whilst its thirsty owner made irritable gestures with his arms to attract Renie's attention.

Suddenly the street door swung open to reveal a powerful gorilla of a man with luxuriant black side-whiskers, a reddish face and small bloodshot eyes which glittered suspiciously as they probed the layers of smoke in the public bar. He took three long strides into the room, fixed Renie with a penetrating stare and advancing his face to within a couple of inches of hers, growled: "Boars'ead!"

Immediately I was reminded of the story of the rather timid landlady who had just come to East London from a quiet country pub and, faced with a similar pronouncement, she shouted nervously; "Pigface yourself !"

Renie was made of sterner stuff and remained quite undaunted by this unusual greeting. She lifted a tin of tobacco down from a shelf behind the bar and staring the gorilla straight back in the eyeballs, she asked: "How much would you like, darling?"

At the other end of the bar a seaman from the

"Hackney" was holding his own little circle enthralled with his reminiscences of a voyage to Greenland on an Arctic trawler. I overheard him say, "We'd gone ashore to git some stores from the village, an' we thought we'd foller the road leadin' inland for a coupla miles, to see what sort o' country it was. Well me an' my mate was jus' comin' to a sharp bend in the road when we stopped dead in our tracks cos o' what come rahnd that corner ....." He paused for a few seconds to allow the drama of the situation to make its proper impact, and two or three of his listeners inquired tremulously what HAD come round the corner?

"A 'uge brahn bear, as big as the Bank o' England" he replied succinctly.

Presently Dick and I said goodnight amidst a chorus of "See you temorrers" and "Mind 'ow you goes". As we emerged into the dark night outside I looked up at the sky and noticed that Limehouse Lil was smoking away happily amongst the stars, quite oblivious to the puny mortals scurrying home around her feet.

The Norwegian sailing-ship 'Christian Radich', passing our house.

Chapter VII

Bonfire Night

In the year 1504, Sir Thomas More wrote an idyllic description of the parish of Stebenhithe, now Stepney, to his friend Dean Colet; "Wheresoever you look, the earth yieldeth you a pleasant prospect; the temperature of the air fresheth you, and the very bounds of the heavens do delight you. Here you find nothing but bounteous gifts of nature and saintlike tokens of innocency."

In another description of this area about the same period I read that there were farmhouses scattered about, an abundance of orchards and gardens, lovely woods, broad pastures and acres of waving corn. Apparently the citizens of London had the right to hunt and fish in these lovely surroundings, which were said to be full of wild birds and creatures fit for human consumption.

It takes a wide stretch of the imagination to picture such a landscape amidst the spider's web of shabby old streets and tall tenement houses of the Borough of Stepney in the twenty-first century. But for all that, some parts of it still have a strange and illusive beauty of their own.

There is a pentagonal strip of waste land close to our house which is bounded by Narrow Street, Ropemakers Fields, Brightlingsea Place, Oak Lane and the Barley Mow Estate. For several years it has served as a rough playground for the children and dogs of the neighbourhood, an exciting sort of jungle landscape where wild flowers and hummocks of coarse grass mingle freely with broken milk bottles, unwanted sofas and old iron bedsteads. Some while ago the Council

The remains of the old boatyard in Newell Street and St Anne's Church.

made arrangements for the whole area to be enclosed within a new corrugated iron fence, with a view to tidying it up and making it inaccessible as a dumping-ground.

The morning after the completion of this operation one could not fail to notice that there were already several chinks in the armour; in fact no less than four substantial strips of that shining silver metal was missing. And no sooner had the bell at Cyril Jackson School rung to announce closing time, than the whole place was inundated, as if by a swarm of locusts, with scores of noisy laughing children scampering about all over the waste land in a frenzy of high spirits and that irresistible sense of freedom that comes at the end of a school day.

Among the first to appear round the corner of Brightlingsea Buildings were a group of Indian children who lived with their parents in a flat right opposite to our house. Mr Lal Singh was a large and impressive Sikh, and when

his wife's sari caught fire while she was cooking the supper one night - a fatal accident that took place with the speed of lightning in front of her youngest children – he wasted no time in replacing her with Sheila, a beautiful girl selected for him by his mother in India.

Lucky and his little sister, Rani, became our special friends, and they soon appeared on our doorstep to discuss serious arrangements for November 5th, the one and only bonfire night in those far off days.

A week or so later, a delapidated engineless car and an ancient three piece suite had mysteriously joined the rest of the flotsam and jetsam on the strip of waste land.

All through the month of October there seemed to be an increasing surge of activity around the abandoned car, and as the days drew in and darkness fell soon after the school bell had rung, there was a certain quality of suppressed excitement in the air. Muffled shouts and infantile threats or words of

Top: Lal Singh from Brightlingsea Buildings, dressed for a special occasion.
Bottom: Lucky Singh (our special friend) out on the Thames.

command flew backwards and forwards across the all-absorbing structure which was arising round that obsolete vehicle.

"Gimme that long plank, Bert, an' 'urry up abaht it or we'll 'ave your Ma bawlin' aht o' the winder!"

A diminutive red-headed child lurched across the hummocks of rough ground with a six foot plank balanced precariously on his frail little shoulders, and several pairs of willing hands grabbed it from him and trundled it into an upright position against the chassis of the car. A large mound, in the shape of a wigwam, was gradually increasing in height and circumference, but certain snags had arisen amongst the foundations which were not proving as robust as the children had anticipated.

The light was rapidly failing and it was becoming more and more difficult to continue the building operations. Suddenly a thin dark-haired girl carrying a flickering torch was seen to approach the site from the direction of the Barley Mow Estate. Immediately a wave of suspicion and hostility rippled through the group round the car, and their leader glared at the newcomer unpleasantly and enquired in a surly tone of voice: "Whatcher pokin' yer big nose over this side o' the fence for?"

"It ain't none o' yer business as fer as I can see," she replied defensively.

"Tha's wha' you fink, is it? Well, fuck orff, you fucking spy," the gang shouted in unison, and six small pink tongues shot out of six angry mouths and pointed towards her diminishing figure as she began to run back home.

There were several serious setbacks before the mound had reached the required proportions, and the worst fears of the building team were soon to be realised when a gang of boys from the new flats on the Barley Mow Estate crept over the fence under cover of darkness one night and set fire to the sacred pile. Before school next morning a tragic group of children had collected round the charred remains, many with tear-stained faces and tightly clenched fists. Luckily the car itself, which formed the core of the whole structure, was still comparatively intact; and that same evening the builders were hard at work once more. One noticed a defiant look about the way their eyes flashed from time to time and a stubborn set to the normally soft contours of their infantile chins. And every night they devised a system of watch-keeping to guard the new mound from all marauders.

One foggy afternoon at the beginning of November I noticed the vague outline of a man, possibly some unidentified father, creeping stealthily across the waste-ground towards that antique heap of metal, carrying an old tin can in one hand. He made a small gap in the pyramid of logs, planks and odds and ends, squeezed the can through this aperture until it was poised on the back seat of the car, then carefully replaced all the outer superstructure. He glanced guiltily over his right shoulder as he drifted silently away into the gathering mists.

The fifth of November dawned a cold and frosty morning, with a huge orange sun rising serenely out of a whitish-blue sky. I set off early with Texel to do the shopping in Salmon Lane, and I chose the short cut across the waste ground in order to make a final inspection of the sacrificial pile. It looked magnificent in the pale autumn sunlight, a miniature Matterhorn encrusted with sparkling white particles of hoar-frost; a fitting monument to the man who died for such a dramatic cause nearly four hundred years ago.

The children from Brightlingsea Buildings and their magnificent bonfire on the waste ground.

Around five o'clock that same evening the underground stations and buses disgorged the usual crowds of homing workers, but they had a sternly purposeful air about them as they sped along the darkening streets. The Limehouse ones made straight towards the waste-ground which was already swarming with tiny figures darting to and fro in a frenzy of last minute preparations, or staggering towards the mound under the weight of some immense burden. It reminded me of an ant heap on the move, motivated by a sort of electric tension which filled the whole atmosphere with waves of excitement.

By the time Jimmy Jones and his children and Dick and I arrived on the scene, the tall mound covering the old car was well and truly alight; flaming tongues of fire shot skywards into the cold black night, then gave birth to a score of burning embers which came drifting back to earth like a torrent of golden rain. There were dozens of children dancing round the fire, their eyes wide with excitement and their lungs emitting piercing shrieks of fear or pleasure as each new firework was set alight by one of the more courageous members of their gang.

It was a strangely primitive scene, that ritual bonfire in the heart of Limehouse. I looked about me and saw the Abraham children, their copper-red hair glittering in the firelight and their mother trying to keep an eye on the whole brood as well as little Susie Bryan, who had brought her white mouse along to see the fun. All the Randall children were there as well, leaping about like scalded grasshoppers as some teenage boy ignited a series of jumping-jacks around their legs: and the Indian children, Lucky and Rani, their dark eyes gleaming with excitement in the gathering dusk.

Out of the dark shadows surrounding Brightlingsea Buildings came a little party of three; a tall serious-looking boy in a blue and white jersey who turned out to be Peter, the one who loves our dog so much; and holding his hands, one on each side, were Johnny and Vera, his young brother and sister. Peter had just left school and started his first job at Lyons near the Tower of London, and I had a distinct impression that he was feeling very grown-up and responsible that evening. When Dick put our box of fireworks on the ground and moved away to look for a spot to set them alight, Peter hurried towards us and said that he would take charge of the box. He hinted darkly that it wasn't safe to leave anything unattended round these parts, for not everyone was to be trusted by a long chalk. So Peter kept an eye on the box, whilst Dick and Jimmy set to work igniting the fireworks. When the first Roman Candle went up there were gasps of wonder and exclamations of "Cor! Ain 't it luvly," from all sides; Peter looked at it with a smile of rapture on his face and observed, "That's a sore sight for eyes, that is!" He was so pleased with this phrase which had rolled off his tongue so smoothly, that he repeated it several times with ever-increasing emphasis. His seven year old sister, Vera, looked up at him with adoring eyes and murmured something appreciative in her deep husky voice, which sounded very comical coming from such a small girl.

Jimmy's children could hardly contain themselves as he set light to a Catherine Wheel, followed by a Treble Rocket. But poor Jimmy himself looked rather forlorn and depressed; as each new firework went off with a resounding bang he announced dismally: "There goes another pint of bitter."

Suddenly there was a surge towards the bonfire. The tin can, which was filled with paraffin, had caught fire and the flames burst out through the windows of the old car, seeming to reach as high as the very top of Limehouse Lil. Meanwhile that venerable vehicle crackled and groaned and rumbled in its final stages of collapse.

About the same time, a tall Jamaican boy ran across the waste ground carrying a monstrous-looking guy over his left shoulder. Its face was made out of a white cabbage, with pellets of coal for eyes, matchstick nostrils and lips carefully etched in fuchsia-coloured lipstick. It was wearing a battered old trilby, with a few strands of brown wool protruding from under the brim to indicate its hair. And it was dressed in an extraordinary assortment of shapeless old garments; a torn tweed jacket over a purple jumper, some baggy grey flannel trousers and a pair of prehistoric snow-boots lined with what was once the pelt of an undernourished rabbit.

A hush fell over the waste ground as the boy approached the bonfire, and I heard a small whimpering noise just behind me. 1 looked round and saw Mrs Collins with her five children clustered around her. The baby, Sean, was asleep in her arms, but little Tracey was shivering with alarm as she looked at the boy with the guy. She hid behind my skirt for the time being, peeping out, first from one side then from the other, like a baby rabbit watching a weasel from behind a tree.

There were more shouts of excitement as the effigy of Guy Fawkes was thrown into the heart of the bonfire. The flames grew hotter and brighter for a few seconds, and his eyes turned into burning coals which illuminated his whole face with a weird incandescent glow. Perhaps it was just a quirk of the imagination, but I could have sworn that I saw a fleeting expression of agony and pleading in those red-hot eyes, before the ugly cabbage face disintegrated into a hundred charred cinders.

Suddenly a cold wind came wafting in from the stealthy black river; icy gusts funnelling between the tall warehouses which fanned the flames of the dying bonfire in a half-hearted attempt to rekindle its former savage vitality. It gave no more than a brief respite from the chill menace of the winter's night which was rapidly settling over London.

Little Tracey began to cry, and Vera's teeth were chattering as she and Johnny searched for their big brother amongst the crowd. All over the waste ground family groups were drawing their coat collars up round their necks and hurrying across the frosty rubble towards their homes. And high above them, as remote as the Great Bear itself, Limehouse Lil was smoking away happily amongst the stars, oblivious to the shivering mortals scurrying around her feet.

Rani on a boat in Battersea park.

Chapter VIII

The Queen of Wapping

"However did you come to live in a ghastly place like Limehouse?" asked the girl in the transparent jade-green dress. "I mean it's full of opium dens and drunken seamen and that sort of thing, isn't it? Surely NO ONE actually lives there?"

Dick began to tell her about Lenny, and how he'd noticed some old houses being converted when he drove down Narrow Street in his lorry one day, and how he'd phoned us that same evening... But the girl wasn't listening any more as her roving eye had just alighted on a young stockbroker who was said to be exceptionally well endowed.

We were wedged into the centre of a fashionable Kensington cocktail-party, and the atmosphere was unpleasantly claustrophobic; a small overfurnished drawing-room filled with sixty or seventy people shouting at each other in resoundingly well-bred voices through a fog of Turkish tobacco and the powerful odour of expensive perfumes.

Our hostess skirmished round the outskirts like a destroyer in charge of a convoy, and suddenly we were being introduced to a "charming friend of mine who ADORES yachting. I know you'll have so much in common!"

A plump man of uncertain age, who bore a striking resemblance to a disillusioned basset-hound, pumped our hands in both of his and launched into an enthusiastic account of all the fun he'd had with dear old Uffa and Max and Owen at Cowes last month; and what class did we race and had we met that old joker, Toby, at the Squadron? Dick began to make polite countering noises and I drifted away into an agreeable sort of daydream. I remember reading once that Admiral Evans of the "Broke", who accompanied Scott to the Antarctic as a young man, said he sometimes felt a mute fool at race meetings, society dinner-parties and dances; and the lure of the 'little voices' would come to him at their strongest at such times. And one of his little voices was the memory of the pack ice hissing round a wooden vessel when the rest of the ocean was engulfed in a weird stillness. He said it was caused by the sear of the floe against the greenheart sheathing which protects the little ship, and was a sound well-known to all ice navigators.

I had my own private collection of little voices, and amongst them I included the gentle lapping of waves against a clinker-built hull; the Limehouse barges banging together in the wash of a passing ship, the ice-cream van playing its melodious tune outside the old buildings .... Dick was whispering urgently in my left ear, "For God's sake let's get out of here!"

We took our leave with a few insincere words to our hostess about how delightful it had all been, and a feeling of infinite relief and thankfulness as we sped eastwards along the Highway, which seemed like the broad path to Heaven that evening. Back at home we sat on the balcony for a long while, watching the tall buildings on the Isle of Dogs changing colour as the sun went down behind Tower Bridge. To begin with they were pale rose, sprinkled with a thousand sparkling gems where the setting sun bids farewell to all the west-facing windows; gradually they turned to deep carmine, then a deeper shade of purple and, finally, deepest indigo blue. It was low water and the barges were all aground on the beach. A solitary police-boat crept by in the gloaming and a bumble-bee was buzzing contentedly around our rosemary bush, apparently unaware of the lateness of the hour. It was one of those sort of evenings when one can sit and do nothing in a profound and companionable silence, feeling serenely happy to be alive and together, in that particular place at that particular time.

The dark shadows along the Rotherhithe shore had already begun to draw out across the still waters when I started to think about my own first introduction to East London, a few months after the end of the Second World War. I had just been demobbed, as a Leading Wren Stoker, from a naval base in the Portsmouth Command; and set off with an ex-Wren friend, Sue Huish, to explore the London River east of Tower Bridge.

We were both wearing bell-bottomed trousers, seamen's jerseys, duffel-coats and woollen caps, and I had taken the precaution of secreting my seaman's knife and marline-spike inside my coat, as we were slightly apprehensive as to what we should find when we emerged from the underground at Wapping, into the heart of that unplumbed and possibly hostile territory known as the East End.

The whole adventure had been inspired by a book which my mother gave me when I was lying in bed with measles at the age of twelve. "The Romance of London's River" was beautifully illustrated by Frank Mason, R.I., and from it I learnt that there were warehouses full of elephant's tusks in Wapping, gigantic Russian timber ships in Lavender Pond and oriental cafés filled with almond-eyed Chinamen in Pennyfields. Also there were names in that book which called out to me in loud clear voices: names like Marigold Stairs, Shoulder of Mutton Alley, Pickled Herring Street, Nightingale Lane, Limehouse Causeway, Cherry Garden Pier and a score of others all waiting patiently to be explored.

I had to wait eight long years before I had a chance to visit those realms of infinite romance; but when the time was at last ripe to go east on my first journey of exploration, I was rewarded with something far more enthralling than I had ever dared to hope for.

Sue and I soon grew to love the old cobble-stoned streets flanked by tall dark warehouses, with numerous little bridges running across the streets about forty feet up in the air, which connected the warehouse ports with their hinterland. Then there were the tantalizing smells of cinnamon, nutmeg and vintage wines coming from those ancient piles, and glorious whiffs of wet timber on a rainy day in the Surrey Commercial Docks.

There is a verse from a poem of John Masefield's which always conjured up for us the magic of the warehouses-

"You showed me nutmegs and nutmeg husks,
Ostrich feathers and elephant tusks ....
Cinnamon, myrrh, and mace you showed,
Golden paradise birds that glowed,
More cigars than a man could count
And a billion cloves in an odorous mount
And choice port wine from a bright glass fount,
You showed for a most delightful hour,
The wealth of the world and London's power."

Between those tall warehouses Sue and I discovered a number of worn old staircases leading down into the river. Amongst the ones we liked the best were Pelican Stairs, Marigold Stairs, Hermitage Stairs and Ratcliff Cross Stairs, from which some of the famous Elizabethan explorers had set off on their voyages to the northern seas. And another of our favourites was Wapping Old Stairs, where a set of decayed and mossy steps shamble down the side of a high wall, several feet above the new stairs which have taken over their duties.

We visited all the riverside pubs east of Tower Bridge, we ate chop suey with real chop-sticks in Pennyfields and we sat for hours in Shadwell Park, entranced by the everlasting pageant of shipping. There were tugs attached to long strings of barges, fish-carriers hurrying upriver to Billingsgate, long ugly flat-irons taking coal to the Fulham gas-works, a rusty Spanish freighter with a cargo of oranges from Bilbao, and a lighter being skilfully manoeuvred across the tide by a couple of men with long sweeps. But the finest sight of all was a Thames sailing-barge with its gigantic tanned mainsail, tacking up to Tower Bridge against the last of the ebb.

London River was living up to our most romantic dreams, but so far it was only peopled by friendly bargees who shouted "Whatcher, Blondie!" as they swept by on the fast-flowing tide, or cheerful warehousemen who wolf-whistled at us from their sky bridges, far above our heads. It was a dream world which lacked a certain reality, until one memorable evening in the autumn of 1946.

* * * * * *

A sailing-barge alongside the Prospect of Whitby in Wapping, in the old days.

The Prospect of Whitby, named after the collier brigs from Whitby which used to drop anchor in the Lower Pool only a few cables away from the balcony, was still a local Wapping pub in those days although it had begun to attract quite a number of visitors from other parts of the world. The landlord, Jimmy Saunders, wore emerald-green shirts and shared his glasses of créme de menthe with a large green parrot which sat on his shoulder; but despite these eccentricities one felt that his heart belonged to Wapping, and he placed the interests of his local customers above those of some of the more affluent ones from the West End.

One evening Sue and I were sitting on a wooden bench in the public bar listening to the little Hawaiin band playing some of our favourite tunes, when I noticed a group of four people seated at a neighbouring table drinking tankards of ale. The two men in the party were having an animated discussion about shipping matters. I overheard the odd phrase like "neap tides next week", "old Sammy dahn at Gravesend", "bloomin' Sun tugs", "load o' cement up Barking Creek", etc. Although they were only fragments in the hubbub of conversation, they fell like music on my ears which were twitching in the manner of insect's antennae to pick up just such details.

The other members of the party were two rather stout matrons aged about sixty, wearing dark cloth coats over gay floral pinafores. One of them had carefully waved hair confined inside a brown hair-net, and her expression was distinctly querulous and disagreeable. Her companion's face, on the other hand, made me think of the rising sun on a clear morning when there is not a cloud in the sky. Little did I realize at that historic moment, that the woman sitting a few feet away

placidly drinking her tankard of ale was destined to become a lifelong friend of mine who would influence my whole outlook on the East End, and many other things besides.

It is hard to remember after so many years what it was about her that made such a special impact at our first encounter. I think the two things which struck me most were her eyes and hands: She had clear cornflower-blue eyes from which shone an extraordinary mixture of childlike innocence and the infinite wisdom of someone who has struggled hard all her life and achieved a complete understanding of the frailties of the human race. Also there was a hint of laughter in the corners of those eyes, and they lit up in the most delightful way when the band began to play her favourite song, "Moonlight and Roses".

Her hands were broad and strong, and looked as if they had worked hard since earliest youth; and she wore an exceptionally wide gold wedding ring on her left hand. But the unusual thing about those hands was the way they lay in peaceful repose on her lap all the time instead of patting the hair, picking the nose, fiddling with something on the table or fluttering in mid-air like neurotic butterflies, the way so many people's hands behave.

'The Queen of Wapping' from a painting by Dennis Ramsay in 1964.

Suddenly the band struck up the opening chords of "Knees Up Mother Brown". The four people I had been watching with such interest rose in unison and, forming a small circle at one end of the bar, they started to dance. Simultaneously the woman with the cornflower-blue eyes beckoned urgently to Sue and me to come and join them.

My word, they could dance those four, and sing too! Sue and I felt like poor anaemic creatures, lacking in vitamins and stamina, when we tried to hold our own in that merry prancing circle. The rhythmic raising of the knees, chin high, the dominant stamping of the feet and the powerful rendering of that fine old Cockney song-

> "Knees up Mother Brown, knees up Mother Brown,
> Under the table you must go, Ee-i ee-i -ee-i -oh,
> If I catch you bending I'll saw your leg right off,
> Knees up, knees up, don't get the breeze up,
> Knees up Mother Brown."

That was how it all started, and I shall never forget the excitement of being included in that tribal dance for the first time, the exquisite sensation of being on the edge of a new world which I desperately wanted to become a part of, even if not a very convincing part.

Introductions were made, and we discovered that the woman with the special eyes was called Mrs Lucy Durrell and her husband, whose name was George, was a small thin man with a cheerful kindly expression and another pair of intensely blue eyes. He was a docker and the other man, who had a strong square face and was called Albie Oates, worked on a tug on

the river. The fourth member of the party, Mrs Mary Heath, was a neighbour and drinking companion of theirs, who always shared the same table in the Prospect of Whitby. I seem to remember that Sue and I were rather vague and not entirely truthful about where we lived and what our jobs were. 1 was living in South Kensington at the time and doing practically nothing whilst Sue was in the middle of a course at the Cordon Bleu. We felt that none of these facts quite fitted in with our image of the sort of people we wished to impersonate, so we glossed over the details as best we could and concentrated on our pasts, when we had both worked hard on boats for nearly three years.

After that memorable evening we were invited to take a glass of beer with our new friends whenever we visited the Prospect of Whitby. At first we stayed in our original seats, on the right of the door as you entered the Public Bar; but, little by little, we began to join the group at their own special table. As soon as our heads appeared round the swing door Lucy Durrell would spot us and begin to beam like an oriental sunrise; then she would make emphatic signals to us to come over and drink with them, having

Charlie, Lucy, Minnie and George Durrell on the beach below the Prospect of Whitby, in the late 1940s.

already dispatched her husband to the bar to buy our black and tans. Mrs Heath usually greeted our arrival with a scowl, but Albie Oates always gave us a broad smile of welcome, and got up to forage for chairs for us to sit on.

During that winter we had some splendid evenings in Wapping. I have no recollections of people getting drunk although the pub was always full at the week-ends; but the sound of all the Wapping people singing the old Cockney songs, so that you could hear them as far away as the Tower of London, was something I shall never forget; and the tribal dancing, that inimitable Cockney sense of humour and the open-handed generosity. I soon began to base all my opinions and knowledge of the East End way of life on Mrs Durrell and her husband and friends, little realizing that she was quite unique in her own special way.

It was a period of extraordinary contrasts in my life. My mother had insisted on my doing the season, although I was twenty by then and considered far too old by most of the other girls I met at dances and cocktail parties. My début at Queen Charlotte's Ball was an experience of unsurpassable horror, and then there were all the country week-ends which made Wapping seem very far away indeed.

My father had recently inherited an immense Victorian pile of a certain rather magnificent grandeur, set amidst countless acres of parkland and forest. The first time I went there, when it still belonged to a very Victorian great-aunt, it left a disturbing impression of butlers and footmen creeping silently around in crepe-soled shoes and a sinister old house-keeper with a bunch of keys dangling from her girdle, who always made one feel EVIL even if one's thoughts were as pure as driven snow at that moment. Any stranger observed wandering through those rural policies was viewed with dark suspicion, and hurriedly dispatched upon their way.

My mother had done her best to liven the place up and dispel some of the putrefying gloom, but I still had to cope with the neighbours one met at local hunt-balls, pheasant-balls and fish-balls, and the eligible young men who proposed marriage because they admired my parents' acreage, although they deplored my point of view. It was a very different world to Wapping, and one in which I felt strangely lost and ill at ease.

Sue and I made the acquaintance of quite a few of the Wapping people once we were firmly established at the table on the left of the entrance at the Prospect of Whitby, and I often noticed that Mrs Durrell was treated rather like a queen by most of the locals, although her language was far from regal if anyone behaved badly in her presence or became too cheeky for her liking. A few terse comments from her tongue were enough to cause the biggest and boldest of men to hang their heads and watch their manners as long as they remained within earshot of our Lucy.

At the end of all those memorable evenings Sue and I would walk from Wapping to Tower Hill Underground Station, along the dimly lit cobble-stoned streets, under all the little sky bridges, pausing for a few seconds near Morocco Wharf to sniff avidly at the glorious scent of cinnamon coming from a neighbouring warehouse. Whenever a ship's siren called out from the river we would run down one of the dark slippery staircases between the tall buildings in the hopes of watching it manoeuvring into the London Docks.

Many times the road bridge was up about the time of high water, with some salt-encrusted freighter inching its way across Wapping Wall to a quiet berth inside the docks. The whole business seemed enormously exciting to us with the dock-master shouting orders, the ship's telegraph ringing urgently and the steady throbbing of powerful engines deep down in the bowels of the ship. There would be figures in long black oilskins pacing the decks impatiently, or peering sternly into the gloomy darkness ahead. And I would begin to dream of the wide open sea and the feel of a deck under my feet, lifting to the ocean swell...

By the time we arrived back at South Kensington, having prepared a suitable alibi for coming home so late, the whole evening would have faded into an aura of unreality which made us wonder if it had ever really happened.

After a few months Sue finished her course and went home to live with her mother near Winchester. This was a bitter blow for me, but I knew enough people in Wapping by then to pluck up courage to go there alone from time to time. And I was invited to bring my mandolin on certain special occasions by Alfie, the leader of the 3-piece band which enlivened the pub with such magic tunes.

Alfie played an electric guitar, Len played a Spanish guitar and Les a ukelele; and I was often allowed to join the

Len, Les and Alfie, with whom I somtimes played my mandolin with their little band at the the Prospect of Whitby.

group when they were playing an Irish medley consisting of some of my favourite songs.

One afternoon the following summer I was invited to 'come round home for a cuppa tea' by Mrs Durrell, after we had been to watch some of her grandchildren marching round the streets of Wapping in the annual St. Patrick's School procession. It was a great privilege to be asked back home in East London, and for me it was the beginning of a new experience; the introduction to a tribal way of life in which the codes of behaviour were far stricter than in most other layers of society. George and Lucy Durrell lived in a ground floor flat, Number 39 Riverside Mansions, and as soon as the procession was over I found myself in the middle of their living-room being introduced to my Dicky, my Ada, my Charlie, my Fanny, my Johnny, my Cissie, my Minnie and scores of little boys and girls and a few more distant relatives.

There was a mountain of ham, salmon and cheese sandwiches, plates full of fancy iced cakes and bowls of pickled onions and pickled gherkins; and Lucy made it her business to see that I was looked after like a princess. No sooner had I taken a few sips from my tea-cup and a couple of nibbles out of a sandwich than I was being admonished for not eating enough and her daughter-in-law, Ada, was ordered to pour me out a fresh cup of tea. Because I was an only child, the sensation of being part of a huge family gathering was quite foreign to me, and I felt very shy amongst so many new people; but they all did their best to make me feel at home as I was, I believe, the only outsider amongst them. I remember thinking that Lucy Durrell seemed like Mother Earth, seated in the best armchair surrounded by all her children and grandchildren; her word was law, and woe betide anyone who attempted to defy her. There was no Victorian atmosphere of fear and repression such as I remember in my grandfather's household when I was a child, but Lucy Durrell's personality and lung-power happened to be more forceful than those of any of her offspring. From that day onwards I began to feel like one of the family. It was during that same summer that we became involved in an extraordinary adventure which welded the ties even further.

I had recently become the proud owner of a converted ship's lifeboat called "Imp", and one Saturday in August I invited Mr and Mrs Durrell, Mrs Heath and Albie Oates to come for a trip down the river to Southend with me. I started from Putney early that morning, and embarked my passengers at Shadwell some two hours later. I had also brought an owl in a cardboard box along with me. It belonged to an ex-Wren friend of mine called Winkle, and she had been looking after it for some weeks, ever since she found it lying half dead in a ditch with one of its wings

Me bringing 'Imp' up the Thames.

A typical street in Wapping sixty years ago.

broken. As she was due to join us at Gravesend that evening for the return voyage upriver, she had entrusted her owl to my care for the day.

We had a cheerful enough trip down the river. The weather was fine and the men drank beer and sang sea shanties, whilst the women laid out a sumptuous banquet on the engine cover. A pleasure steamer, also heading for Southend, whose skipper was a mate of Albie's, invited us to accept a tow-rope somewhere near Tilbury Docks. This resulted in our reaching our destination sooner than we had anticipated, so some of the party decided to go ashore there to sample the pleasures of the land.

The flood tide had been making for several hours and the warmth had gone out of the sun by the time we set off on our return voyage to Gravesend. It was suggested that Albie should take the tiller, as he knew all about the river and the places where you could find the best run of the tide round certain sharp bends.

Towards sunset we were passing Chapman Light, which used to guard the shoals off Canvey Island. Albie said he'd take us over near the Kentish shore as we should find the ebb, which had already started to run, was much weaker on that side. No one demurred, for we all felt secure in Albie's hands; after all it was his river, that he worked on, year in and year out.

I was inside the cabin trying to light the stove to make a cup of tea when it happened. There was a tremendous jolt, and the "Imp" shuddered from stem to stern as we ran decisively aground on the Blyth Sand, close to a desolate-looking spot called St. Mary's Bay. The engine roared in protest whilst the propeller churned itself to a standstill in a bed of glutinous black mud. There was another three to four hours of ebb still to run before the tide would turn, and I calculated that we could not hope to find ourselves afloat again before about 3.30 a.m. next morning.

Having spent much of the previous four years, since leaving school, aground on various sand-banks in a variety of different boats, it did not strike me as being a matter of great importance. Just one of those tiresome misadventures which happen to the best of us at certain times; something to be viewed with a calm detachment and fatalistic resignation. The only thing which did rather worry me was the thought of poor Winkle sitting on the end of the Royal Terrace Pier at Gravesend, waiting patiently for our arrival; but I thought she would probably guess that we had run aground.

Albie, who was after all responsible for our present situation, treated the whole affair as a huge joke, and George Durrell seemed inclined to take his side. But the two women became extremely alarmed as darkness fell, and Lucy Durrell was very anxious about her Ada who would certainly be waiting up for them, with no means of discovering what had become of them.

Albie and George wrapped themselves up in their overcoats and tried to get some sleep in the cockpit, whilst the rest of us sat huddled together in the cabin which was tilted at an extraordinary angle towards the Essex shore. Owing to this fact, it was impossible to light the stove to make a hot drink and we had already eaten all the provisions we had brought with us for the outing. To add to our discomfort, the one and only bucket which served a rather essential purpose, had fallen overboard during the excitement of the grounding and been swallowed up by the all-absorbing mud.

All day long I had tried feeding the owl with tasty titbits of meat, but he had turned them down with a shake of his large feathered head and a long pessimistic stare from his round yellow eyes. Then I had made the cheering discovery, during our short interlude at Southend, that he liked a drop of whisky! I was so anxious that he should not feel homesick and miss Winkle too much, that I fed him quite a few teaspoonfuls of this beverage, until he became rather comatose and settled his head snugly on his left shoulder to go to sleep.

It must have been sometime around midnight, when we were all dozing fitfully in the cabin, that the owl arose in his box and uttered a deep-toned booming noise which sounded like "Hu-hu-hoo", followed by a long wild shriek, interlarded with hissing, snoring and yapping notes. He stood on tiptoe inside his box, extended his unbroken wing and flapped it energetically for some minutes. At the same time his yellow eyes flashed fiercely in the candle-light.

Mrs Heath began to scream, which excited the owl still further, and Mrs Durrell gripped my arm and appealed several times to the Almighty to preserve us. Even the men called out from the cockpit, to ask what the racket was all about.

The middle of the night is certainly the one period in the whole cycle of twenty-four hours when an owl sets out to enjoy himself. Gone were the sleepy, rather endearing gestures of the daytime. Our bird was wide awake, and he continued to boom and screech and flap his wing in such a strident manner, that I was quite unable to think of any way of soothing him. I could only conclude that the uproar in which he was indulging was either some form of mating call, or the results of a monumental hangover. My textbook about British birds had recommended a diet of small rodents, insects and occasional tiny birds, but as this was out of the question in the middle of the Blyth Sand, and the mating opportunities were not very favourable either, there was little we could do to improve the situation.

At last the flood tide came in from the sea and a cold wind came whistling across from the Essex marshes, lifting the tops off the small black waves which were just beginning to slap against the clinker-built hull of our stranded boat. What with the wind and the waves and the owl, none of us were sorry to feel the "Imp" lifting to the swell once more, and I was particularly relieved when the engine started and we were able to get under way.

Gravesend lay sleeping in the cold grey light of dawn when we moored up alongside a tug at the Royal Terrace Pier. There was no sign of Winkle, and the owl had fallen asleep at last. I said that I would wait there until she turned up, and the Wapping contingent were to go home by train as originally planned.

Mrs Heath was the first up the ladder, muttering something about "that fucking bird" as she disappeared from sight on to the jetty. But when it came to Mrs Durrell's turn, she didn't want to leave me there alone and tried to persuade the others to stay on. I assured them all that I would be perfectly alright, and in the end the two men dragged her up the ladder as Mrs Heath was creating quite a disturbance up at the top.

I watched the four of them moving slowly along the pier,

and when Lucy Durrell looked back to wave goodbye there were big tears rolling down her cheeks.

Winkle turned up in rather a state some five hours later, as her night had also been far from uneventful. She had waited at the end of the pier until about midnight, then, having decided that we were unlikely to turn up that night, she had sought out a policeman and asked him where she could find somewhere inexpensive to sleep. He had recommended her to follow him, and taken her to a home for girls of dubious morals. The door was already locked and bolted behind her before she realised what sort of place it was, and they refused to release her until 10 a.m. next day!

However, the expedition to Southend ended happily enough. The owl perked up enormously once he was reunited with his owner, and we had a very pleasant voyage up the river to our moorings at Putney.

The whole adventure made a resounding impression on the Durrell's friends at the Prospect of Whitby. Each time I met them there, Lucy Durrell told the story to a wide-eyed audience who hung on her every word; and I'm bound to say that the story grew and grew in the matter of perilous dangers overcome, as the months rolled by. 1 shall always remember her final dramatic statement at the end of each telling, which was; "That boat did everything bar sink!"

Albie was perhaps the only one present who knew as well as I did that a boat aground on a sand-bank can't possibly sink, but he never let on in front of the others; he would just flutter an eyelid imperceptibly when I was looking that way, then puff away contentedly at some particularly vile-smelling brand of tobacco he favoured at that period.

Chapter IX

The Invincible Ones

It was not until a good many years later that I learnt something of Lucy Durrell's early history and the prodigious struggles she had had to keep her family above water.

In the days when she was young, Wapping and Shadwell were very different places to what they are today. The Ratcliffe Highway, known as the Regent Street of sailors, ran through the middle of the two districts and it was a street of ill repute filled with low drinking dens, dance-halls, brothels, cheap cafés and wild beast shops, the yards of which were packed with lions, tigers, hyenas, wolves; in fact any animal in demand amongst the keepers of menageries. Some were known to have as many as fifteen lions in stock at one time. The sailors just home from abroad would go to those extraordinary places to sell their pets and barter curiosities.

The Ratcliffe Highway had also been the scene of the brutal murder of two entire families in 1811, and its unsavoury reputation lingered on until most of the street disappeared during the bombing of the East End in the Second World War.

In Wapping itself, prosperity had begun to decline during the early part of the nineteenth century when the ships of the East and West India Companies first started using the new docks in Poplar, instead of anchoring out in the river off Wapping. Their cargo was then carried direct to the City along the newly constructed Commercial Road and, as a result of this, Wapping was cut off and gradually lost its former importance.

Before the London Docks were opened in 1805, it was estimated that some ten thousand thieves preyed on the cargoes of the vessels moored in the open river, relieving them of about £500,000 of goods each year. This amounted to less than 1% of the total value of the cargoes handled in the port of London in those days.

There used to be two hundred or more riverside pubs between Tower Gateway and Frying Pan Stairs, but many of these were gradually replaced by a wall of fortress-like warehouses which shut out the southern sun from the hinterland of Wapping. The ship's captains and prosperous merchants sold their large houses and left, and these became cheap lodging-houses run by rack-rent landlords, who herded the Irish emigrants and seamen just home from abroad into their evil abodes, to live in the most appalling conditions.

Shadwell, which was Lucy Durrell's original home, had changed rather less. The church of St. Paul's, Shadwell, known as the Church of the Sea Captains and made famous by Captain Cook who was married to a local girl there, stood sentinel over an important cross-roads on the Ratcliffe Highway; and all the open spaces in the parish were used as rope walks, where the immense cables for the ships were twisted by the ropemakers. Cable Street derives its name from this practice, and so does Ropemakers Fields, leading off Narrow Street.

The rest of the parish was occupied by ship's chandlers, biscuit bakers, boat-builders, mast and block-makers, sail-makers, anchor-smiths, rat-catchers and pawnbrokers; in fact, most of the inhabitants drew their livelihood from the bustling trade of the river or docks.

Lucy's father, Mr Lazzam, must have been one of the few exceptions as he was a chimney-sweep. He was Italian by origin and he married an English girl who gave birth to seven children. His favourite daughter, Lucy Annie Leah, was born in 1885. Mr Lazzam was a very strict father who ruled his family with a rod of iron. When Lucy was a child it cost a penny a day to go to school, so her parents could seldom afford to send her. As soon as she was old enough she took a job as a shop-girl, and because any sort of work was often hard to come by in those days, the hours were long and the pay very poor.

Lucy was still a young girl when she met and fell in love with a fish-porter from Billingsgate. He had ginger-coloured hair and was called George Durrell. He soon asked her to marry him but she dared not tell her father; he must have had his own suspicions however, for he sought out the lad on his return from work one evening and roared at him: "You keep your hands off my Lucy, you ginger-headed devil!"

With the connivance of her mother, Lucy married her George in secret the following day. The marriage turned out a complete success, and they lived happily together for more than half a century afterwards.

George and Lucy Durrell started their life together in two rooms in an old building in Solander Street, which was situated between Cable Street and the Ratcliffe Highway. The tenement houses in Shadwell in the early part of the century were mostly bug-ridden old dwellings where large families were crowded into one or two rooms, with a communal cooking-stove and lavatory shared between several families. Only a minimal amount of fresh air and daylight penetrated the small windows which often faced similar tall dark buildings on the other side of a dirty courtyard. Lucy gave birth to eight children during her years in Solander Street, but times were so hard that she often had to work all night at Badger's, the jam-packing factory in Stepney, then go home to look after her babies during the daytime.

When the First World War started George Durrell joined the army, and he was sent out to India some weeks before another baby was due to be born. He arrived in Bombay on the same day that she arrived on this earth, so she was always known as Minnie Bombay by all her family. When George returned to London at the end of the war he became a docker, but his wages were only five shillings a day if he was lucky enough to find any work. There was no Welfare State to look after the people in those days, and Lucy must have had a dreadful struggle to make ends meet. However, there were very few things that she could not turn her hand to and one of the numerous seasonal jobs that she did, year after year, was shelling peas at Baxter's in Leadenhall Market.

Early in their married life the Durrells lost three of their children, and when two of them died within a couple of days of each other there was no money left to bury the last baby. Lucy was beside herself with grief to think that she could not arrange a proper burial for one of her children; but a younger brother of hers stepped into the breach at the last moment and gave her the money for the funeral, a loving gesture that she never forgot in later years.

Cissie, who was the eldest remaining daughter, sometimes recalled the reputation that her mother had acquired in those far off days in Solander Street. If anyone in the buildings was feeling ill or miserable, or in some sort of trouble financially, Mrs Durrell was always the first one to help them out. She would think nothing of sitting up all night tending the sick, or lending her week's wages to someone whose need she felt was greater than hers. She had a way of finding out all about a person's troubles without having to ask them any questions, then doing her utmost to help them. Her generosity was boundless, and she always expected the best in other people and refused to become disillusioned.

By the time Minnie had reached the age of sixteen the Durrell's circumstances had just begun to improve, and they moved to a new block of flats called Riverside Mansions on the edge of Shadwell Basin in Wapping. All the Guinness ships from Dublin used this small dock, and there were always rows and rows of barrels of Guinness along the quays on either side of the basin.

Although they were living in a new flat with much more space and modern conveniences, Mrs Durrell missed her old home in Solander Street for a long while. Wapping was foreign territory, even if it was only ten minutes walk from her native Shadwell; and it seemed a long way to Watney Street Market which has always been the very heart of Shadwell. However her five children grew and flourished, and it was not long before her eldest son, Charlie, had met a girl called Fanny, also living in Riverside Mansions, who was soon to become his wife.

At last Lucy Durrell began to settle in and her husband's wages gradually increased. The skies were certainly looking brighter, and by the time I first became acquainted with them all their children were married and living nearby on the island of Wapping. It really was an island, for it was bounded by the River Thames to the south and by St. Katherine's Dock, the London Docks and Shadwell Basin to the west, north and east. And the inhabitants were true islanders who resisted all tempting offers from the housing authorities to rehouse them on new estates in other parts of London or Essex. For them, there was nowhere else on earth as beautiful and desirable as the ancient hamlet of Wapping, and places like Piccadilly Circus or Trafalgar Square seemed

as remote as Timbuctoo or the upper reaches of the Amazon. Why there was even a pea-shooter lady, who woke them each morning in time to go to work by shooting peas at their windows till they roused themselves from their beds!

Every year, during the month of September, thousands of East Enders used to travel down to the Weald of Kent for the annual hop-

Mrs Smith, the Queen of the Pea-Shooters, one of the last knocker's-up in East London.

Down hopping at Horsmunden in Kent.

picking season. It was no rest cure for they had to work in the fields from dawn till dusk each day, filling their individual bins with the juicy green hops in order to make enough money to pay for the whole expedition. But it was a grand way of life all the same, and for most of them the only change of air they were ever likely to get. For three or

Lucy and me in the late 1940s.

At George and Barbara's wedding in Wapping in March 1960. Auntie Anne, Minnie, Lucy, me, Junie, Ada, Dennis and Johnny, with Tina, Marie, Terry and Martin at the front.

four weeks the families lived in rough wooden huts close to the farmhouses, and after a hard day's work, they would meet in the village pubs or sit around their bonfires singing lustily under the stars.

The Durrell family always went to the same farm near Horsmunden, and on several occasions I went down there for the day to join them. George Durrell would walk up to the railway station to meet me and escort me back across the village green and down a long country lane to the farm where they worked. On arrival I usually found Mrs Durrell seated on a low canvas stool outside their hut, tending some tasty concoction in a huge black cooking-pot which was suspended from a tripod over a wood fire. Her daughter, Minnie, and daughter-in-law, Ada, were always near at hand to fetch and carry, and once the meal was ready the whole family would gather round the fire with their bowls and spoons. Sometimes there were twenty of us there on a Sunday, and when we had finished eating someone in the group was sure to say, "How about a song now?"

Suddenly the lush green meadows would resound with the stirring words of:

"Dai-sy, Dai-sy,
Give me your answer do!
I'm half cra-zy,
All for the love of you!"

and some of the other families who worked on the same farm would take up the refrain, until there were scores of voices all roaring in unison:

"It won't be a styl-ish mar-riage,
I can't af-ford a car-riage,
But you'll look sweet
Upon the seat
Of a bi-cy-cle made for two!"

I always returned to London from these excursions laden with bunches of hops and carrier-bags full of apples procured for me from a neighbouring orchard by Lucy's young grandson, Georgie, who had inherited his grandfather's ginger-coloured hair.

It so happened that Georgie's wedding was the first of a series of splendid Durrell weddings to which I was invited some years later. They were tremendous unforgettable occasions, sometimes lasting for two or three days at a time with the Queen of Wapping, as I had come to think of her by then, presiding over the whole tribal ceremony, her entire family around her and a smile of intense enjoyment illuminating her round pink face.

Lucy Durrell had never learnt to read or write but her wisdom was infinite, and each week when all the family earnings were brought to her she decided exactly how they should be layed out to the best advantage.

There were some very sad times in the saga of the Durrell family in the 1950s. First George Durrell, Lucy's husband, died and a few years later her eldest son, Charlie, was drowned in one of the docks. Her life was never quite the same after that accident, although she was blessed with the sort of buoyant nature and calm philosophy which could weather the worst of storms.

In 1965 Dick and I were invited to Lucy Durrell's eightieth birthday party. She had twenty-eight great-grandchildren by then, so there were plenty of willing hands to pull her out of her chair when we all began to sing "Knees Up Mother Brown...". It was a party in the old Durrell tradition, and the Queen of Wapping sat in her favourite armchair smiling happily with her hands lying peacefully in her lap as they had always done. Whenever someone started to sing one of her special songs, a few tears would roll down her cheeks as she joined in the chorus.

Mrs Durrell's youngest daughter, Minnie, and all her family were at the party, and Dick told them that we should love to live in East London if we ever decided to leave the country. At that time he was working as a G.P. in Ashford, and we were living in an old Kentish farmhouse at Pluckley.

About two years later, when we had seriously decided to move to London, it was Minnie's brother-in-law, Lennie Smith, who rang us up one evening to say that he had noticed some old houses being converted into flats in Limehouse, and had stopped in his lorry to make some enquiries on our behalf from the workmen. And they had advised us to get in touch with a Mr Magnus Bartlett, who might be persuaded to rent us part of his house. So that was how we first came to live in Limehouse, through a far-reaching chain of events which had started on that unforgettable evening more than twenty years ago.

* * *

Our visitors to our house in Kent: Dick, Ada, Minnie, Dickie, Marie, Johnny, Cissie's husband, Lenny, Cissie, Anna and Junie. Summer 1966.

Chapter X

Cyril Jackson School

When we first came to live in Limehouse, I could just see the roof of Cyril Jackson School from our kitchen window. It was a dark-red Victorian building surrounded by much of the waste land caused by bomb explosions during the Second World War. If you crossed Narrow Street and walked due north along Brightlingsea Place till you came to Northey Street, the school arose importantly on that corner, with only a narrow passage called Oak Lane to link it with the waste land and St Anne's Church further east.

My first interview with Mr Palmer, the Headmaster, took place in a stuffy little office on the third floor; and I found myself boasting to him about all the work I had done as a school-care-worker in four other schools in Islington – I had to make a good first impression at all costs, I told myself.

Mr Palmer was a dedicated Headmaster and not easily taken in, but he agreed to give me a trial. The date of the next school medical examination was then entered into my diary, and I was told to arrive punctually, meet the doctor and school nurse, and sit at a desk writing notes about all the children who had medical problems. And I would be required to visit many of those families in the weeks ahead to make sure that they had been to various dental and vision clinics; and if not, why not? Also there was the question of Children's Country Holidays, a throw back to the war years. For those who had been recommended by the doctor or headteacher, it was necessary to fill in a form giving sometimes embarrassing details of their family circumstances; but I soon became acquainted with many of the so-called problem families living around us.

*   *   *

A year or two later the school moved to a new and very smart open plan building at the southern end of Three Colts Street. It had extensive playgrounds, and the Cyril Jackson football team soon became well-known for their skill and determination.

In those days there was always a neighbourhood policeman, either on foot or horseback, to keep an eye on the school and its children. It caused great excitement one afternoon when he brought his horse into the playground to meet the children from the Infant's Class.

Mr Palmer retired in due course, and a powerful Headmistress whom we all addressed as Marion took his

Two children from the Cyril Jackson school and me, sailing back to Limehouse from Tower Bridge.

place. She was always very keen on some of her children, the ones who had a particularly sad or restricted home life, getting away from London and inhaling the fresh country air or, better still, spending a day beside the sea. And when she heard that I owned a sailing-boat on which I had been teaching a group of boys in long-term care for several years, she soon produced four pupils in her top Junior Class whom she felt would benefit greatly from this experience.

Mrs Ebbs, a teacher in the Junior School, volunteered to join me, and she and I and our two dogs began travelling to Walton-on-Naze by train once a week with four boys, Simon, Mark, Jonathan and Paul. We had some great times sailing on the Walton Backwaters and out to sea off Harwich, and studying seamanship and navigation. And on our way home to Liverpool Street, each of the boys filled in their log-books and wrote a short account of what they had seen and learnt during their short voyages. Simon, a little half-Irish boy with a wonderful sense of humour, wrote the finest accounts of all, some of which I still have to this day.

* * *

There was a big surprise in store for me one winter's day in 1980, when I was paying my weekly visit to Cyril Jackson School.

"We have a lady here who has just come from Hong Kong," the school secretary told me; "and she would like to have a few words with you?"

We met over a cup of tea in the office, and the lady

from Hong Kong, whose name was Beverley West, told me that she had been out there working for several years, trying to help the Chinese boat-people who had escaped from Haiphong in North Vietnam. Some of them were drowned at sea because their boats were so unseaworthy, but the ones who did finally reach Hong Kong were in serious need of someone to take care of them. She and some friends had formed a rescue centre in which they housed a number of families, helped with all the paperwork required to allow them to emigrate to England, then brought them to another rescue centre at Hothfield in Kent where they would spend a further year till they could be found more permanent accommodation and schooling for their children.

The Ngoc and Quan Anh with their 8 children, and Tito and me, on our balcony soon after their arrival in Narrow Street. About 1980.

Quan Anh and her children with Peter Cobb and his daughters in Battersea Park.

One such family, The Ngoc and Quan Anh Mac with their eight children, had just arrived in Limehouse, and they had been housed in an old block of flats at the eastern end of Narrow Street; and all the children of Junior and Infants school age were to attend Cyril Jackson School.

"I will take you to meet them today if you can spare the time?" Beverley fixed me with a hopeful gaze. "They are a charming family and I have to return to Hong Kong very soon and would hate to leave them without a friend to turn to. Only one speaks a little English, and they are very shy."

There was no escape from this one I soon realized, as Marion, the Headmistress, had just looked in to say how much she admired the work done by this visitor for the wretched boat-people who had been forced to flee their homes.

Bich Ha was the first member of the Chinese family who opened the door of their flat in Garford House, and greeted us with a big smile and a few words in English to invite us indoors. I noticed that there were numerous pairs of shoes in the narrow entrance hall, and it soon became clear to me that everyone removed their shoes on arrival so as not to soil the new carpets provided by Social Services.

The mother, Quan Anh Mac, brewed some Chinese tea, and I was soon being introduced to a few of the other children who had just returned from school. They had many problems to deal with: emigration papers, schooling, getting on to medical lists, learning English, shopping if they had any money to spend; and Bich Ha was the only one to guide them into this strange new world which Mother and Father clearly found quite alarming.

After my first introduction I used to visit the Mac family every week, and sometimes we would go on excursions to Hampton Court or Greenwich Park or St Katherine's Dock; and Dick made their acquaintance for the first time when they all came to tea in our home. They were such a lovely family, and we were devastated when we heard what had happened on their first Christmas in Limehouse. Father The Ngoc and all his children went out for a short walk, and Mother stayed at home to prepare the lunch. A few minutes later three men wearing masks burst into the flat and stole every small treasure that they had managed to save and bring to England; even a small wrist-watch that had belonged to her father. It was a terrible blow from which it took her many months to recover.

Phuc and Bich Ha's wedding day.

Another year passed, and I found myself driving Dick's car, with red balloons attached all around the roof-rack, and Bich Ha with her fiancé, Phuc, inside. They were going to their wedding at Stratford Registry Office, and all the people who knew that red was the colour for joy and celebration in China, cheered as we drove slowly along Stratford Broadway.

After Bich Ha's wedding came her sister, Nguyet Ha, and gradually all the sisters and brothers married boys or girls from their own country; and some years later there were numerous little grandchildren who attended Cyril Jackson School.

Chapter XI

Bugsby's Hole

"They might accept you, on the other 'and they might not," observed Postie non-committally. "All depends 'ow toffee-nosed you are, see what I mean?"

We saw what he meant quite clearly, and before going back into the long wooden hut which was warmed by a charcoal stove at one end, we made a determined effort to detoffeefy our noses. The three of us were standing on a platform outside the Greenwich Yacht Club overlooking Bugsby's Hole, and we were conversing in hoarse whispers befitting the climatic conditions around us.

It was a bitterly cold night at the end of February, and the river was enshrouded in a dense grey fog which muffled the steady thumping of ship's propellers out in Bugsby's Reach and blurred the silhouettes of the low buildings strung out along the edge of the muddy foreshore. Even the lights inside the club-house shone with a mysterious orange glow, opaque pools of brightness in the all-embracing murk.

Postie was a small friendly type of man whose nickname meant exactly what it implied; he was a Greenwich postman who owned a small and homely-looking vessel which he pointed out to us with great pride amongst the ghostlike shapes recumbent in the thick black mud beneath us. She was about eighteen feet long and very pointed at the end which was intended to cleave through the waves, whilst the other end was chopped off severe and square. A structure which resembled a miniature triangular greenhouse arose defiantly above her narrow decks, and Postie explained to us that he had the finest accommodation bar none on this side of the river, for you could stand upright inside the cabin, cook yourself a tasty meal, have a good kipper in a comfortable bunk, and there was even room to keep a few potted plants up the for'ard end and a dog's basket for his little bitch, Rosie, to sleep in near the stove.

"If it wasn't for that ole motor bein' a bit dodgy, I'd be orff acrost the Atlantic and suchlike," he told us with a deep-throated chuckle.

Dick had recently become the owner of a twenty foot fishing boat called the "Beagle", and he was very anxious to find a berth for her on the River Thames, not too far from where we live. According to our five hundred year lease of 88, Narrow Street, we were the legal owners of the mooring rights directly below our house; but Mrs Woodward Fisher's

barges were emphatically in total occupation there, and short of cutting them adrift one dark night when there was a strong ebb tide and a westerly gale blowing, we could think of no method of dislodging them. Mother Thames was not disposed to listen to any reasonable propositions on the score of our joint mooring rights.

Mother aboard the "Beagle" heading upriver.

135

Then, one marvellous autumn afternoon, I found the Greenwich Yacht Club. It was the sort of day which is created solely for exploration and discovery. The wind was strong and pungent, there were big white cotton-wool clouds sailing serenely across an azure blue sky and the river was intensely alive; a moving mass of olive-green water, flashing gold and silver darts out of its swirling tide-rips, with a cavalcade of freighters, tugs, barges, pleasure-craft and half-submerged logs moving steadily downstream on the ebb. I even caught a fleeting glimpse of the immense tanned sails of an old Thames sailing-barge tacking across Bugsby's Reach, at the far end of River Way.

River Way is an offshoot of the Marsh in East Greenwich where George, the foreman at Woodward Fisher's, was born and bred. There is something rather special about that little street which it is hard to place a finger on, some indefinable charm which you could search for in a thousand other by-ways and not be able to find. For one thing it is a region of bold strong outlines, unsoftened by any human foibles like front gardens or window-boxes. There is a miniature pub called the Pilot attached to one end of a row of four-roomed cottages and then, in magnificent contrast, all the big stuff. On the west side grows an outcrop of tall silver chimneys belonging to the South Metropolitan Gas Works, which pierce the summer sky like a group of Viking warriors advancing into battle in by-gone days; and a little farther along stands the enormous black chimney of the Blackwall Point Power Station, rising majestically above the wall at the far end of River Way. On the east side of the street are the offices and sheds of Redpath Brown and Co. Ltd. and, finally, Tate and Lyle's sugar factory, crouching like some prehistoric monster on the northern horizon.

When the wind is in the right direction as it was that afternoon, there is a unique and all-pervading smell in River Way, a rich odour composed of the outpourings of a score of variegated chimneys; the gas works, the United Molassine Co., Vim's Dogfoods, the Greenwich Saw Mills, Tate and Lyle's over in Silvertown and the river smells wafting in from Bugsby's Reach.

Bugsby's Reach! That was the real heart of the matter. I have never discovered exactly who Mr Bugsby was, although a book I once read about the Port of London hinted that he may have been the owner of an extensive region of market gardens lying inland from the big loop of the river which now bears his name. Be that as it may, his memory is perpetuated by a number of other places such as Bugsby's Hole Barge Roads, Bugsby's Hole Stairs, Bugsby's Hole Causeway and Bugsby's Hole itself, a sheltered haven of rich black mud where small craft can lie in safety, undisturbed by the turbulent waters farther out.

A *Thames sailing-barge running upriver.*

I turned right at the far end of River Way and walked along a tow-path where rose-bay willow-herbs and giant dandelions flourished amongst the tufts of coarse grass on either side of the path. Presently I came to a pair of long wooden huts with a board outside them announcing that this was the Greenwich Yacht Club. On the steps of the further hut sat an old man who glared at me in a most ferocious manner; despite this discouraging reception, I felt a surge of uncontrollable excitement and pleasure as I surveyed the rows of small boats rolling happily to and fro on their moorings, and the broad expanse of the river beyond, flowing down towards Woolwich Reach and the wide open sea. The very wind was laden with the scent of briny exploits, so I hurried home to share my thrilling discoveries with Dick.

Time flowed by and it was not until the following winter that we went together to Bugsby's Hole and stood on the edge of the river trying to picture the "Beagle" secured to one of those moorings, bobbing up and down in the swells from passing ships or resting in a bed of soft mud at low water. The whole idea appealed to us enormously, and as the boat was many miles away at Woodbridge in Suffolk at that time, we felt an impatient urge to make the preliminary arrangements with all possible speed. These, however, proved to be more intricate than we had anticipated.

Dick approached the old man, who was still crouching on the club-house steps like some medieval watch-dog. He glared mistrustfully at my husband, cast a few venomous glances at our dog, then swivelled round to focus his bloodshot orbs on me. Suddenly they glittered with the light of recognition, but no pleasant smile of welcome illuminated his rugged old face; he merely looked more ferocious than ever before.

"Wha'd'yer want?" he growled at Dick, half rising from the steps to defend the interior of the Greenwich Yacht Club against all invaders.

"I want to know how I can get in touch with the secretary of the club, about joining it and finding a mooring for my boat?" Dick replied, in his mildest and most persuasive voice.

"Tuesday night, rahnd 'alf seven," the old man barked, pointing with a gnarled forefinger at the entrance to the second hut. Then he drew himself up to his full height of about five feet, and secured an immense padlock to the door of the hut outside which he had been sitting, thereby emphasizing that the interview was over and that he was perfectly 'au fait' with the tricks of all casual prowlers like us. Dick and I retraced our steps at a brisk pace along the tow-path, feeling more like a couple of criminals on the run than two prospective members of the Greenwich Yacht Club.

Undeterred by the apparent impregnability of the club, we returned to Bugsby's Hole again the following Tuesday evening. On this occasion we were greeted by the most charming man called Mr Everett, the club's Commodore, who went out of his way to make us feel at

Dick with Texel, motoring along the Thames estuary in the "Beagle".

home. He introduced us to a handful of members, amongst them Postie, who were warming themselves round the stove, and he explained that our names would be put up on the notice-board if we wanted to become members; however, he suggested that it would be a good idea if we came along on Tuesday evenings whenever we could so that some of the others could get to know us before the next committee meeting, when our fate would be decided by the number of votes in our favour.

It was soon after this that Postie took us outside, ostensibly to show us his boat, but also to warn us how not to behave if we wished to become members of the oldest yacht club on the river. I believe it was during our third Tuesday evening at Greenwich that we made the acquaintance of the harbour-master, who was in charge of all the moorings along the foreshore. He was a man of weighty opinions who took his job very seriously indeed, and Dick had been most anxious to meet him in the hopes that he might allow us to have a mooring for the "Beagle" eventually, if we were accepted as members of the club.

He came in rather late, wearing an immense pair of mud-caked thigh-boots and carrying a length of rusty old anchor-chain over his right shoulder. The first thing he noticed was Texel, who was having a tug-of-war over a torn brown sock with Postie's little bitch under one of the tables, and causing a lot of amusement amongst the spectators. The harbour-master was not amused, and by the time his beetling brows had reached a high enough elevation to allow a pair of glacier-blue eyes to focus on us, we began to squirm in our seats under the searchlight quality of his appraisal.

After greeting one or two people and accepting a cup of tea from the Vice-Commodore's wife, he strode over to where we were sitting and, without any gentle preliminaries, growled at Dick: "I saw your names up on the board to be considered at our next committee meeting. Well I don't know anything about you, do I? So there's no reason why I should vote in your favour and let you into our club, is there?"

The wind was sucked right out of our sails by such a fierce and unexpected onslaught and we were left tossing in the swell, so to speak, and temporarily bereft of the valuable powers of speech. The harbour-master gulped down his tea and strode out into the night with his anchor-chain still suspended over one shoulder. As soon as the door closed behind him the Vice-Commodore's wife, who was a most amiable and sympathetic woman, set about trying to comfort us.

"You don't want to mind what he says too much" she

Dan, Sailor and Dick outside the Greenwich Yacht Club.

exclaimed in a soothing voice, "for his bark's always been worse than his bite!"

A chorus of murmurs of agreement came from the group around the stove.

"But if you want him to give you a mooring, you'll have to handle him with great care," she warned us. "Never try and rush him as he's the type of man who can't stand being rushed. He knows his business alright, and these moorings are what he lives for, in a manner of speaking; but you've got to let him arrange things in his own good time, if you see what I mean?"

We thanked her very much for her valuable advice and promised to bear it in mind if we should ever succeed in joining the club. But our earlier hopes were tinged with pessimism, what with Sailor, the old man on the steps, to guard the premises by day, and the harbour-master there to keep an eye on the more frivolous members of the committee who might feel inclined to vote in our favour.

We did not return to Bugsby's Hole for the next few weeks, as we were busy fitting out the "Beagle" to go to sea. Then the letter arrived, one sunny spring morning at the beginning of April. It was from Mr Everett to tell us that we had both been elected members of the Greenwich Yacht Club, and the committee wished to extend to us a hearty welcome. He also suggested that Dick should contact the harbour-master as soon as possible, as he knew how anxious he was to find a mooring for the "Beagle".

The sun seemed to shine with a special brilliance the following Sunday as we strode triumphantly down River

Way and along the tow-path in search of the harbour-master. Even Sailor treated us to a fleeting contortion of the facial muscles which we took to be a smile, and gave us permission to look inside his hut, under strict supervision. It proved to be the sort of place to delight a mariner's heart. There was a carpenter's bench, a vice, a battery charger, various masts and spars under construction, bits of prehistoric machinery which were being resuscitated with considerable optimism, two long benches on either side of the hut, an old stove at the far end with a kettle chirruping happily on top of it, and a selection of vast and rather grubby tin mugs grouped around a teapot of no mean proportions. It was a real corner of paradise for the sailors of Bugsby's Hole; a place where you could spend a pleasant hour or so tinkering with some invaluable piece of gear from your boat; where the talk was slow and soothing, about ships and the river, and the tea was strong and potent, a fitting beverage for those who had struggled mightily against wind and tide on the turbulent waters of the Lower Thames.

Presently the harbour-master joined us in Sailor's hut and agreed, rather reluctantly, to give due consideration to Dick's request for a mooring. I was longing to pin him down in some way and shout at him "When, WHEN shall we have our mooring?" But I managed to keep my tongue under control, and we both behaved as if time was no object and next year would do just as well as this year over such a trivial matter as to where to keep our boat.

Meanwhile the "Beagle", herself, was gradually creeping nearer to the River Thames, for we had set off on our maiden voyage from Woodbridge at the end of March; on Good Friday to be precise.

It had not been easy leaving the River Deben on account of George Jones. His brother had designed the "Beagle", and their joint boat-building firm, Beagle Boats Ltd., had been responsible for her construction the previous year. But a whole summer and autumn had intervened since she first took to the water, and during that time she had cast her spell over George Jones to such an extent that he was extremely unwilling to part with her, and had placed every conceivable impediment in our path to delay our departure. Mind you, I could see his point, for there WAS something rather special about the "Beagle", although she was no sleek-lined yacht of aristocratic bearing.

She was, in fact, a clinker-built motor-boat with a broad beam and large open cockpit suitable for hauling in trawl-nets full of North Sea fish. She had larch planking on oak frames, and the larch had been carefully selected from a coniferous plantation somewhere north of the Thames, as George Jones assured us that these were far superior to the ones grown in Southern England. Her cabin was of reddish-gold mahogany, with two real brass-rimmed portholes on either side, and it formed a complete triangle in which two pairs of feet were apt to jostle each other for supremacy of position at the for'ard end of the two bunks, which met in the shape of a V near the Samson's post. There was a small galley department with a Swedish cooking-stove at the head of the port bunk, and a locker in which to hang oilskins on the starboard side. The whole concern was far from spacious, but despite all its disadvantages it contrived to look unexpectedly warm and cosy inside.

A small mast was stepped on the cabin-top, which could support a gaff-rigged loose-footed mainsail and a tiny jib under moderate conditions of wind; but the real motive-power of the boat was a 6 H.P. Sabb diesel engine, which was situated in the centre of the cockpit. This piece of machinery was Dick's pride and joy, and a triumphant grin would spread across his face after the complicated rigmarole of starting up had been successfully achieved and the familiar choomph, choomph noise was causing the whole boat to shudder with eager anticipation.

It was not until the evening of Good Friday that we finally made our departure from Woodbridge under cover of darkness. George Jones had been hovering around all day, showing us this and that, recommending Dick to manoeuvre the boat thus and so, and generally preventing us from unpacking and settling down to make our personal acquaintance with the "Beagle". At the latest possible moment he rushed off home to dine in the bosom of his family; no sooner had his shadow disappeared round the corner of the shed than we released the mooring-ropes, dropped downstream on the ebb for a few hundred yards in total silence, then Dick started the engine and we chugged along the river to Ramsholt where we dropped anchor amongst a cluster of small craft. It was a clear frosty night with a million stars in the sky above us, and the music of the fast-flowing tide chuckling happily around our clinker-built hull. There was a heavy dew on deck and the air was bitterly cold, but inside the cabin it seemed as warm and comfortable as a thrush's nest.

Early next morning we emerged from the River Deben rather nervously, but the weather forecast was good and the "Beagle" sped down the coast of Suffolk in fine style with her engine running smoothly and her sails set to steady her in the beam sea. We felt reassured, for it was clear that she could take to the open sea as easily as the proverbial duck takes to water.

Luckily it was not until we reached the mouth of the River Blackwater some hours later that the north-east wind suddenly freshened to Force 6, causing a most alarming sea in the estuary with the wind against tide. As soon as the flood started to run we sped up the river under jib alone, with foaming yellow waves hissing in a menacing way round our stern. It was not an encouraging sight, but the "Beagle" seemed to take charge of us and she brought us safely into Heybridge Basin about the time of high water.

On Easter Sunday it was blowing a north-easterly gale so we decided to stay put. However, during the course of the day we came across various families living aboard rotting hulks who were said to have entered the basin twenty years ago and never left it since. This filled us with intense gloom and despondency, so we decided to move out on the evening tide at all costs.

That night the "Beagle" took us to Maldon and selected a pleasant quay stacked with timber where we were able to spend a quiet night. Then the wind dropped completely, so we set off about 5 A.M. and motored past Osea Island at the hour of sunrise. The whole river was clothed in a soft white mist and suddenly we saw the little island suspended halfway between earth and sky, like the mirage of an oasis in the Sahara Desert. And as if that was not enough glory for one morning, a Baltic trading-schooner which lay at anchor off the eastern end of the island loomed up ahead of us like some beautiful dream-ship.

It was the last day of our short Easter holiday, so we sped down the river, turned sharp right through the Ray Sand Channel, then sharp right again into the River Crouch. Once the mist had cleared it became a real North Sea morning with an olive-green sea quivering restlessly under a broad apple-green sky; the gulls cried raucously to each other in mid-air and the wind smelt of seaweed and salt water and the good life out on the open sea. Far-away across the Maplin Sands I could see a number of brown-sailed barges moving serenely down the West Swin towards the Thames estuary.

Later that day we left the "Beagle" on a mooring off Prior's yard at Burnham-on-Crouch, and travelled rather dismally back to London, packed like tinned sardines amongst the Bank Holiday crowds.

It was nearly midsummer before the harbour-master drew Dick aside one Tuesday evening and, pointing to a small space below the club-house in Bugsby's Hole, between Postie's boat and a largish motor-cruiser called "Steady Barker", said that he could keep the "Beagle" there provided he laid his own moorings.

"And I assume you know how to do that small job?" he demanded fiercely, treating Dick to one of his most searching and glacierlike stares.

My husband behaved as if he had spent the last twenty-five years of his life laying out moorings, to the exclusion of all else. He may have overplayed the part a bit, for I noticed a glint of suspicion flash briefly across the harbour-master's face; but he also seemed to be enjoying some private joke which he did not see fit to share with us.

It took us some few days to assemble the appropriate chunks of chain of a suitable length and weight, as well as some huge shackles with which to attach them to the ground-chains. There were to be four chains in all, two for the bows and two for the quarters; and the two for'ard ones were shackled together and secured round the Samson's post by means of an eye-splice, whilst the ones leading to either quarter each had their own seperate loops to slip over the two towing-bollards. It all seemed rather unexpectedly complicated, but we received a great deal of help and guidance from an old sea-dog called Dan who came into our lives about that time.

He was a member of the Greenwich Yacht Club who had retired from active life some years before, and who spent his days sitting on a pile of drift-wood outside one of the huts observing the movements of shipping in Bugsby's Reach with the calm blue eyes of a connoisseur who has spent many years gazing at far horizons. He had been born and bred in Wapping in the days when it was a real seafaring parish, and as a young man he had driven a pony-cart all over the south of England, carrying goods from one place to another and eagerly absorbing the folklore wherever he went.

During his long hours of peaceful contemplation, whilst the tides ebbed and flowed and ships came and went, Dan had evolved a gentle philosophy which was utterly foreign to the bustle and hubbub of modern life.

"Don't you ever feel cold, Dan?" I used to ask, when it was blowing an easterly gale with driving rain and sleet, and Dan was still sitting on his pile of drift-wood facing straight towards Siberia.

"No, never, girl!" he would laugh, with a thousand tiny crow's-feet appearing round his merry blue eyes. "Fresh air's the best tonic a man can git these days. Think of all those poor geezers crouched over their tellies in their stuffy little 'ouses, an' some of 'em even fouled up wiv central 'eating nahadays; whereas I've got more than most millionaires ever git, what wiv the river and all the ships te watch, an' the smell o' the wind commin' straight aht o' the North Sea like this!"

He inhaled deeply and luxuriously, whilst he stirred up some evil-looking concoction in a battered old saucepan and examined it with intense interest from time to time.

"Whatever have you got in that saucepan, Dan?" I asked.

"Me own special brand of 'orseradish sauce, girl," he replied with a chuckle. "Didn't you know that the wherewivall fer makin' it grows along this very tow-path, so you don't ever need te go buyin' it in the shops no more. Scurvy-grass is what the sailors used te call it in the old days, and many of 'em would've given their right arms fer a few 'andfuls of it arter they'd bin beatin' arahnd orff the 'Orn fer a cupla months."

Presently he climbed up the steps and set his saucepan down on Sailor's stove, and the two old men sat alongside each other on the wooden bench watching it bubble and thicken, with a gleam of enormous excitement in their eyes.

The mooring-chains were finally assembled and

placed under the joint guardianship of Sailor and Dan. Having selected an evening when he would have the maximum amount of low water and daylight combined, Dick dressed himself in his oldest jersey and trousers and a brand new pair of thigh-boots to counteract the mud of Bugsby's Hole, and, armed with a short boat-hook, an adjustable spanner and a huge pair of plyers, he started on the all-absorbing job of laying his moorings.

Luckily the harbour-master was not around when we first arrived, and Dan showed Dick exactly where to find the first ground-chain to which he was meant to attach the twin mooring-chains for the "Beagle's" bows. Everything went smoothly enough to begin with, and I had no difficulty in holding the chain up a few inches above the mud whilst Dick shackled on the moorings. In fact it took so little time that we became puffed up with an entirely false impression of our own resourcefulness, so that the second half of the whole manoeuvre came as a nasty shock.

"If you foller along Postie's starn moorin', that should bring you aht to where the second grahnd-chain lies," advised Dan, with a note of anxiety in his voice. Dick strode manfully into Bugsby's Hole, and the mud went glug, glug, glug all around him; slowly it crept up his legs until it had reached a level of less than two inches from the top of his boots and was becoming more and more difficult to wade through. He gripped Postie's stern mooring-line to steady himself, but a few seconds later it came away in his hands, nearly throwing him off balance in the process. This was an unforeseen dilemma, for whatever did or didn't happen about the "Beagle's" stern mooring-chains, he felt morally bound to remoor Postie's boat that evening.

Dick at low water in Bugsby's Hole, doing some work on the "Beagle's" hull

Sailor and Dan shouted advice from the jetty, and Texel and I hovered unhappily on the beach whilst Dick wallowed further and further into the mud. It rose above the top of his thigh-boots and squirmed down inside them like a trickle of icy blanc-mange; it plopped all over his jersey and even found its way into his hair and across his face. I felt quite panic-stricken, standing there uselessly on the beach holding a piece of rope with which to try and lasso him if the worst came to the worst; and I thought bitterly of the harbour-master, harbouring his beastly little private joke like some wicked old gnome the other evening.

In everyday life Dick is inclined to be lazy over trivial matters, and does not exert himself unduly if he can get away with a more leisurely approach to the subject. But on that occasion he scented a direct challenge, and he made up his mind to tackle those stern moorings successfully before the tide rose that evening, whatever the hazards. He waded across to "Steady Barker", wallowed out beyond her stern until he was shoulder deep in mud, then heaved with all his might until he got a grip on that miserable ground-chain. Somehow he managed to haul it back a few feet so that he could work on it close to "Steady Barker's" rudder. All the rest of the business securing Postie's boat and shackling on our two stern moorings, had to be done in total darkness below the surface of that filthy black mud. But he struggled mightily and succeeded in the end, although the tide had crept up to within a few yards of him and the gathering shades of night were closing in round Bugsby's Hole by the time he had screwed up the last shackle.

Arrayed like an African hippopotamus in a solid coating of black mud, Dick turned his back on the river at last and started wading towards the beach. Suddenly he let out a sharp cry of pain for he had trodden on something hard and pointed underfoot. He steadied himself alongside Postie's boat and fished around with the boat-hook to see what it was; and a minute later he brought up an ancient horse-shoe on the end of the hook.

A small audience had collected outside the club-house to watch the laying of the "Beagle's" moorings, and in their midst stood the prominent figure of the harbour-master; a new and gentler type of harbour-master who greeted my mud monster with a friendly smile and offered him a mug of tea laced with rum, which Sailor had freshly brewed on his stove. The Commodore was there too, and I had a distinct impression that Dick had won his spurs that evening and was now considered a worthwhile addition to the Greenwich Yacht Club.

We reached home about 11 P.M. and Dick had three baths, one after the other, whilst I cleaned and sandpapered the horse-shoe, and nailed it to the door of our kitchen.

Gravesend and Tilbury on a busy morning.

Chapter XII

The "Beagle" Comes to Town

Several weeks before the laying of the "Beagle's" moorings had finally taken place she, herself, had crossed the Thames estuary to Harty Ferry on the north coast of Kent.

We returned to Burnham-on-Crouch one Friday evening early in May, then motored down the river on the ebb tide next morning and took the short cut through the River Roach behind Foulness Island. Emerging into the open sea at Havengore an hour or so after high water, we crossed the submerged Roman road over the Maplin Sands with our hearts in our mouths and only a few inches of water under our keel; but the "Beagle", who was obviously accustomed to such risky manoeuvres, never wavered on her southerly course which took us straight down the broad sparkling pathway of the sun.

Away from the Maplin Sands there was a steep following sea and a fresh wind on the quarter which rippled through Texel's fur and made her very unhappy indeed. She is not a brave seafaring dog by any standards, although she tolerates the more luxurious types of yachts when they are firmly secured to a quayside, provided there is plenty to eat on board and ample provision for stretching out in a cool soft place on deck. Unfortunately we are seldom able to provide her with these ideal conditions, so we motored into the River Medway and dropped anchor in Stangate Creek, partly on her account.

On the East Coast, where mud of all colours and textures is the prevailing theme, a place to land on comparatively firm ground is something of a rarity. Slaughterhouse Point, at the far end of Stangate Creek, is one such place, and we rowed across there with our sulky Airedale that evening and strode about on the saltings whilst the dog chased grasshoppers and field-mice, which were small enough to cause no alarm and to make her feel larger and braver than usual.

We spent the night at anchor in the creek, and I remember waking up at 3 a.m. and going out into the cockpit to admire the view. The anchorage was bathed in brilliant moonlight and there were a few small marsh birds calling to each other across the mud-banks. The tide was murmuring a gentle melody around the "Beagle's" hull and away on the northern horizon I could see an enormous tanker moving majestically along the broad reaches of the Medway. It was the sort of night when all the strivings of puny mortals seem as nothing compared with the immense and eternal glory of the universe.

Week-ends are always so tantalisingly short, and it seemed only a few hours later that we left the "Beagle" on a mooring at Harty Ferry, walked up the sweet-scented country lane to

The "Beagle" on her mooring off the Greenwich Yacht Club.

the village of Oare, caught a bus to Faversham, a train to Victoria and the Underground and bus back home.

Three whole months passed by before we finally brought the "Beagle" home to Bugsby's Hole.

That particular week-end there was a copper-coloured sun blazing down out of a cloudless blue sky, and the corn stood so high and golden in the Kentish fields that I had to stand on the "Beagle's" cabin-top to see what lay beyond it. Hardly a breath of wind disturbed the hot August air as we motored along the River Swale to Queenborough, then out of the Medway and into the Thames. Choomph, choomph, choomph sang the little Sabb engine, doing its level best to keep abeam of a Polish freighter sweeping upriver on the flood.

We anchored off Gravesend on Saturday night; always a favourite place of mine with the feel of big ships all around one, the tugs and ferry-boats darting hither and thither, the North Sea pilots strolling solemnly up and down the Royal Terrace Pier and the special smell of the river where it mingles with the wide open sea.

There was a light easterly breeze blowing on Sunday morning, so Dick hoisted the mainsail and jib and we sailed rather splendidly up the middle of Northfleet Hope with the flood tide giving us a good boost in the right direction. There was very little shipping about, but a short while after our departure I noticed a sleek launch with an impressive bow wave coming up astern of us.

"I hope she's got someone at the helm," I said to Dick rather nervously. "She seems to be heading straight for us and she's going at a hell of a speed."

He was sitting peacefully on the stern smoking his pipe and

regarding the set of the "Beagle's" mainsail with an appreciative eye. By the time he turned round, the launch was only about thirty yards astern; and not only was there a man at the helm, but another one up for'ard who was pointing an abnormally large loud-hailer in our direction. It suddenly occurred to us that the "Beagle" seemed to be the object of their pursuit.

Before we could even contemplate starting up our little diesel in the hopes of evading them, the other vessel, which was a P.L.A. harbour-master's launch, swept across our port quarter, thereby shaking all the wind out of our sails and causing us to gybe unexpectedly. Then the man on the bows bawled through his loud-hailer in a harsh grating voice: "Get over to the north side of the river, can't you? You're a bloody embarrassment to shipping, stuck out there in the middle!"

There was no shipping in sight just then, and it was the first time we had ever been called an embarrassment to that particular commodity although we had sailed around all over Northern Europe for some years. But before Dick could open his mouth to utter a suitable reply the launch, which had circled right round us in a showy manner, swung hard to port and, exhibiting a long white froth of a stern wave, made off towards some other miserable speck on the western horizon.

Dick started up his engine with all speed and set off in pursuit, as the chrysalis of a scathing rejoinder was beginning to formulate on his lips. However his opponent was too wily for that sort of game: his top speed was about twenty-five knots whilst ours was six, so he disappeared in a cloud of spray round a sharp bend in the river leading to Fiddler's Reach, and that was the last we saw of him that day.

Presently the breeze died away and a sultry overpowering heat poured down out of the blazing midday sky. We furled the "Beagle's" sails and chugged on up the river, past Greenhithe with the black and white "Worcester" outlined against the green hills of Kent, then up Long Reach, Erith Rands, Halfway Reach, Barking Reach, Gallions Reach and through the busy thoroughfare between North and South Woolwich. At last we came to Bugsby's Hole, and there was old Dan sculling around in a heavy rowing-boat, waiting to give us a hand with those unforgettable mooring-chains.

The "Beagle" swung into position for the final run in between Postie's boat and "Steady Barker". I held my breath and crossed my fingers for there was quite an audience collected outside the club-house, their attention rivetted on our arrival. However there was no cause to worry for the "Beagle" moved gently ahead between the other two boats, and Dan passed the bow mooring up to me from his dinghy whilst Dick grabbed hold of the stern moorings and secured them. The whole manoeuvre had proved unexpectedly easy. Later on that evening Dan rowed us ashore in his dinghy and the "Beagle" settled into the mud beside her new neighbours.

After the "Beagle"s arrival in Greenwich Dan and Sailor vied with each other as watch-dogs, and hardly a day passed without one or other of them rearranging her fenders, taking up the slack on one of the mooring-chains, or moving some of the drift-wood at low water so that she could have the softest possible bed to lie in.

We met Dan walking towards us along the tow-path one evening, and Dick asked him rather anxiously if the "Beagle" was alright as we had not been there since the equinoctial gales set in the previous week.

"You'll find your boat and Postie's lying very sociable just now," replied Dan, with a twinkle in his eye. "But 1 bin watching 'em te see they didn't git up te nuffink they didn't aughta."

A few minutes later we saw what he meant, for the "Beagle" was lying over at a sharper angle than usual and her cabin-top was only about six inches away from her neighbour's gunwale. Postie, himself, seldom put in an appearance at the club any longer as he had conceived a passion for old-time dancing which severely curtailed his nautical activities. However, the "Beagle's" top-sides were festooned with fenders of all shapes and sizes, which Dan had carefully placed at any points where the two boats might make contact. Sometimes I wondered if he stayed there all night, just to make sure that no mishap overtook his charge during the hours of darkness.

The other day I was reading some verses about London River by a lady called Miss C. Fox Smith, and for some reason or other they made me think of Dan, although I doubt if he has ever sailed much farther than the Nore ....

The "Beagle" and Postie's boat 'lying sociable' at low tide in Bugsby's Hole.

"They passed – like summer clouds they passed,
As fleeting and as fair:
The shapely hull, the soaring mast,
The speed beyond compare.
The hemp, the teak, the brasses bright,
The sunlit sails ashine,
The paint, the planking scoured and white,
The spars of glistening pine.
They passed – the ships, the men likewise,
The captains tried and bold,
And rich in lore of seas and skies,
The mates of mighty mould.
The bawling bos'uns heard afar,
Sea craftsmen, 'Chips' and 'Sails',
The crews whose veins ran Stockholm tar,
Big fisted, hard as nails.

And there he sits alongside old Sailor, gazing wistfully
down the river dreaming of those days of not so long ago
when many a glorious vessel came proudly sailing up London
River on the tide, her holds full of wool from Australia, or tea
from China, or fine silks and spices from the Indies.

"You aughta 'ave seen Li 'mus Basin in the old days, girl.
The way they used te stop those great sailin'-ships wiv the
checkin'- posts, when there was a fresh wind blowin' acrost
the river. They'd take a turn rahnd the post wiv a good
strong bit o' rope made fast te the ship's starn, and when the
rope tautened up it'd pull 'er up sharp like a restive 'orse
when the old bit gits a grip on 'is mouth. Sometimes the
rope'd eat right through the wood on the checkin'-post, on
account o' the strain bein' so great; I've even seen them

posts set alight by the friction of a brand new bit o' manilla!" His gentle blue eyes followed the progress of a little tramp steamer heading towards the mouth of the River Lea, but they still shone with the light of reminiscence:

"Wappin' ain't anyfink like what it used te be when I was a lad," he continued; "I can recall the time when there was thirty-six beer shops along Wappin' 'Igh Street and Wappin' Wall; lem'me see, there was the Ship'n'Pilot, Ship'n'Star, Ship'n'Punchbowl, Union Flag'n'Punchbowl, the Gun, North American Sailor, Golden Anchor, Anchor'n'Ope, the Ship, Tahn o' Ramsgate, Queen's Landin', Ship'n' Whale, Three Mariners and the Prospect o' Whitby. I can't recall the names of all the others, but they was all good seafarin' pubs, they was. And then there was Paddy's Goose up the 'Ighway, where the girls used te git up te some right old capers.

"Wappin' was fall o' boat-builders, rope-makers and ship's stores in those days, and a man oo knew a bit abaht gardens and suchlike come dahn there one day and 'e sees a red flower in a pot, what one o' the sailors 'ad fetched 'ome from the West Indies, in a ship chandler's winder, so 'e goes in and buys it; when 'e gits back' tome 'e takes some cuttin's orff of it, and the next year 'e sells 'em for a guinea a piece. And that was 'ow the first fuchsia come to England!"

Early in December I went along to Bugsby's Hole one afternoon to invite Dan to our Christmas party. Sailor was in hospital at the time, and I found our old friend sitting by himself on the steps of the club-house, making a monkey's fist out of an odd bit of hemp. When I had issued the invitation a look of profound uncertainty and alarm spread across his face, and his normally serene blue eyes wore the expression of a hunted animal.

"I've never bin one fer socializin'," he mumbled in a gruff sort of voice. "Always left that sort o' caper te the sister; you know what women's like? Dressin' up and all that lark. Can't sit still fer a moment she can't, So I even went aht and bought 'er a telly te try and anchor 'er dahn a bit. The last time I wore a shirt wiv a collar'n'tie was two years back, come Januwerry, and that was fer me mate's funeral, that was,"

He hadn't exactly refused the invitation, so I tried some different tactics in my most dulcet tone of voice: "How about bringing your sister along too, Dan, if she enjoys a party like you said? And there'll be lots of friends of ours from Wapping and Limehouse coming to it, so you might find someone you used to know there?"

At the mention of Wapping I thought I detected a flicker of indecision in his troubled eyes, a momentary weakening of the defences he was building up against our party.

There was a long pause and I looked away down Woolwich Reach to where a rusty old coaster in ballast was plodding upstream against wind and tide. The river was yellow and beige that afternoon, and the dark silhouette of the ship stood out in sharp relief against the pale December sky.

Presently Dan drew a long breath of good river air and, clearing his throat experimentally once or twice, he said: "Thanks fer the invitation, girl, but its caught me in irons so te speak. I'll go back 'ome and think the matter over; I might be too busy that pertic'lar evenin', on the other 'and I mightn't be, so I won't say one way or t'other this arternoon."

So we left it like that; and by the time I had reached the far end of River Way the first tentative fingers of twilight were closing in around Bugsby's Hole.

Chapter XIII

The "Thalatta" Affair

Mrs Brown presented a firm bold front to the world at large as she strode into the middle of Limehouse Causeway and brought the heavy lorry traffic to a grinding halt. For a matter of thirty seconds she stood there, foursquare and supreme, the whites of her eyes flashing defiantly in the afternoon sunshine and her staff of office held proudly against her right hip. Britannia in charge of the waves with her trident ready to hand might have stood in just such a way as that.

The roaring bustling everyday life of the neighbourhood paused momentarily, as if to draw breath, and a very small child crossed the road at a leisurely pace, clutching the plastic model of a steam-ship in his right hand. Immense Diesel engines panted like thirsty buffaloes on either hand, but he hardly seemed to be aware of their existence as he sauntered past Mrs Brown, treating her to a fleeting smile of grateful complicity, then turned right in the direction of Three Colts Street.

The interval was soon over and the lorries thundered on their way. Mrs Brown, moved across to the school entrance gate to talk to a friend from her own island of Barbados and Robert, the boy with the plastic steam-ship, ordered a bar of Cadbury's fruit'n'nut from the big woman behind the counter in Bernies. It was a day like any other except for a touch of frost in the air which seemed to evoke a special brilliance in all the Limehouse colours. The warehouses on Dunbar Wharf glowed like water-melons, those on Aberdeen Wharf were flushed with the

tones of vintage burgundy and Bethlehem House had turned the colour of ripe tomatoes; but all these buildings, by no means insignificant in themselves, appeared like puny doll's houses in comparison with the magnificent bulk of Limehouse Lil. She was soaring ecstatically amongst the white cauliflower clouds clustered over the Stepney landscape, and her smoke streamed away towards the northern boundary of the borough, an undulating line of black soot which left its mark wherever it went.

Robert retraced his steps along Three Colts Street, pausing to whisper something in one of the long bedraggled ears of Harry's old pony which was pulling his fruit and vegetable cart slowly towards the Enterprise. The child then turned left at the cross-roads and quickened his pace as he walked westwards along Narrow Street.

Robert was ten years old, although he looked more like a boy of seven or eight; he had green eyes set in a thin white face, a few freckles round the nose and an untidy mop of fair hair. His father was a native of Scotland and a plumber by trade, but owing to a back injury and general ill-health he had been out of work for several years, and had taken up the study of philosophy, antiques and Japanese art.

Above: Mrs Brown, the crossing lady in Narrow Street

Robert's mother was a small delicate Irishwoman who had given birth to six children. She worked tremendously hard all day long and often looked as if she was on her last legs; but, despite all their hardships, they were a close and happy family who accepted their lot in a philosophical manner. And the small flat in which they lived was something to be proud of, combining Jock's good taste and the fruits of his wife's industry; altogether it was quite an eye-opener in a neighbourhood which was not renowned for the beauty of its homesteads.

"Robert's always been the odd one out in our family," his mother once told me. "I can't make him out, he's so different from all the others. You never know what he's going to do next, but he can stand on his own feet orright

The East Coast Sail Trust barge "Thalatta".

even though he's so small"

She glanced at her son with pride and affection, but Jock soon interrupted her to tell me about a Japanese sword he had recently acquired which was going to make him into a rich man as soon as he could find the time to take it along to Sotheby's. His wife fluttered her right eyelid almost imperceptibly, so that only I could see, and urged him to put on the kettle and make us all a cup of tea.

On that frosty winter's afternoon when Robert was heading along Narrow Street in such a purposeful manner, I was busy working at my desk beside the window in Trevor's pad. Suddenly the bell rang and Texel woke up with a start and galloped along the hall, barking furiously as she approached the front door; I followed close behind her and was astonished to see her come to a sudden halt in front of the letter-box, where she continued to bark as noisily as ever although her tail was wagging happily.

"What an extraordinary way to behave," I thought to myself; and then I noticed the letter-box flap was rising slowly and a small slab of Cadbury's fruit'n'nut was being pushed through it from the outside. The dog nearly choked with excitement as she took a grab at the chocolate, then jumped up and down on the door-mat where she attempted to swallow it and continue barking at one and the same time.

I opened the front door and Robert held out the miniature steam-ship which he announced he had brought as a present for me. He explained that the funnels pulled out to hold salt and pepper, and he thought it would look very nice on our dinner-table. I thanked him very much as I held the hot and sticky toy in my hands, and by way of a small return gesture, found myself inviting him to come with me the following afternoon to see an old Thames sailing-barge which was moored alongside Tower Pier. He accepted with alacrity, offered the remains of his chocolate to Texel, then beat a hasty retreat before I should have time to change my mind.

I sometimes wonder who really instigates these nautical escapades, Robert or me? It is true that the original proposal is formulated by me and the words escape from my own mouth, but as a rule I have neither the time nor the inclination to waste a couple of hours on some madcap adventure on the river, until that invisible seed has been implanted in my subconscious mind by some outside agent... One day last summer was a glaring example of what I am trying to explain. Robert came round and asked if I had seen the new hydrofoils which had just started running up and down the river between Tower Pier and Greenwich? I admitted to having noticed them on one or two occasions, and he replied that they didn't 'alf look 'citing, the way they rose out of the water like sorts o' birds and skimmed along the surface in a cloud of spray! I found myself agreeing with him, that they did look rather exciting; and inviting him to come for a trip on one the following week!

Shortly before the appointed day, Robert returned to ask if he could bring a friend along with him. I said "Yes", and the next afternoon, nearly an hour before the time at which I had agreed to take them, he turned up with Herman, a small West Indian boy who lived in the flat above him. That particular escapade was a great success and we all enjoyed our trip on the Thames Arrow Express. And there was a rather amusing incident in connection with it, which has engraved the whole afternoon indelibly on my memory.

We had made the round trip from Greenwich to Tower Pier and back again, and the three of us were strolling past the front of the Naval College on our way back to the car-park. Suddenly we came face to face with a very naval-looking old gentleman who was endeavouring to squeeze past us on the narrow footpath. He glared ferociously at the two boys, treating Herman in particular to the harsh scrutiny of his steel-grey eyes; then he swivelled his attention on to me, and fixing me with a long cold stare he growled "White trash" in a voice which was accustomed to making itself heard above the sound of the wind and waves, no matter how hard it was blowing. Simultaneously Robert, who had run on a little distance ahead, bawled at me; "I want te go te the toilet!"

And he seemed mystified when he noticed that I was doubled up with laughter and quite unable to cope with any solution to his predicament for several minutes.

George Jones, our old friend from Woodbridge who was so reluctant to part with the "Beagle", had become deeply involved in a splendid scheme called the East Coast Sail Trust, which was an endeavour to buy up some old sailing-barges, make them into a seaworthy condition and use them for training the boys of Essex and East London in the ancient arts of seamanship and navigation. After enormous efforts they had acquired enough money to purchase and put in order their first barge, "Thalatta", and

she had just accomplished a highly successful season sailing around the Thames estuary with boys from the Borough of Redbridge as her crew.

The autumn being well advanced by then, the barge sailed up London River to spend a few days alongside Tower Pier. It was an official visit organised by George Jones and various prominent members of the Port of London Authority, and the object was to gain as much publicity as possible for the East Coast Sail Trust in order to raise enough money to buy another barge for the use of the Borough of Tower Hamlets. With this end in view, George arranged a series of cocktail-parties aboard, rather grand affairs at which cabinet ministers, master mariners, eminent clergy, famous marine painters, pillars of the House of Lords and a certain number of lesser fry rubbed shoulders together inside the homely interior of the barge.

On the day that I had invited Robert to come and see "Thalatta" I was unable to leave home before 4.30 p.m.; so we set off in the fading light of a December afternoon, with a dark grey sky above us which gave promise of some early rain. It took a little while to find a free parking meter on Tower Hill and it was after five by the time we reached the pier; and I noticed that Robert was shivering

Above: Limehouse Lil

inside his thin threadbare jacket. I began to regret that I had ever thought of bringing him to see "Thalatta", and I said in a firm tone of voice: "We've only come to have a quick look at the barge from the end of the pier. You mustn't go on board or anything like that; and if you like we'll drive home through the Rotherhithe Tunnel?" This last suggestion was by way of a titbit to make up for the scantiness of the present outing. Robert did not reply; in fact I doubt if he had even heard me for he was hanging over the railings gazing up at the top of "Thalatta's" mainmast, with an expression of rapture on his face.

Presently a hatchway opened in front of us and a pleasant-looking girl wearing a navy-blue jersey and trousers smiled at Robert and asked if he would like to come down and see the engine-room. I opened my mouth to intervene and to say that we had only come to have a quick look at the barge from the pier; but I was too late, as Robert had already nipped aboard and was half way down the iron ladder leading to the engine-room. I shouted rather helplessly at the disappearing crown of his head; "Don't be more than a minute or two, will you? I'll wait up here on the pier."

I waited for five, ten, fifteen minutes..., then it began to rain. I put up my umbrella and marched sulkily to and fro, getting more and more angry the wetter I became. Suddenly a group of people dressed in dinner-jackets and long evening dresses appeared out of the darkness behind me, and clambering aboard with some difficulty they disappeared through the for'ard hatch. Then a plump bishop, arrayed entirely in purple down to the smallest buttons on his gaiters, negotiated the bulwarks and vanished into the bowels of the barge.

1 was becoming quite frantic, one way and another, when a figure in black oilskins climbed out through the after hatch, strolled across to where I was standing and exclaimed: "Good heavens! Whatever are YOU doing standing around in the pouring rain? Why not come aboard and join the party?"

I must admit that I was very relieved to see the cheerful face of George Jones grinning at me from under a dripping sou'wester. Immediately I disclaimed all intention of gate-crashing his party, but explained about the dilemma I was in and asked if he could go in search of the small boy I had lost down the engine-room hatch.

"You don't mean Robert, do you?" asked George, with a peculiar twinkle in his eyes. "It may not be too easy to get hold of him just at present. You see he's having a drink in the saloon right now, and he's in the middle of telling his life story to the Chairman of the Harwich Harbour Board who, I'm sure, would hate to have it cut short!"

"What an extraordinary state of affairs!" I thought to myself, as George moved away to greet a fresh cluster of guests. "Here's me standing on deck (I'd climbed aboard by then) in the rain, and that pestilential brat swilling cocktails in a nice warm cabin surrounded by bishops and chairmen and women in long evening dresses!"

At that moment the brat in question emerged on deck looking flushed and rather guilty.

"Sorry I kept you waitin' so long," he mumbled, as we hurried back along the pier. "But they poured me out a coke then they arst me te sign me name in the visiter's book and there was lots o' people kept arsting me different fings."

I felt relieved that he'd only been drinking coke, and my general irritation began to evaporate when I realised that he'd obviously been enjoying himself.

We were driving along Narrow Street on our way home when Robert suddenly turned to me and said; "There wasn't 'alf a lot o' posh people on that boat. One fing I'll say fer you an' Dick, you ain't posh."

I began to feel quite flattered by this unexpected compliment; then, on further reflection, I wondered if he really meant that Dick and I weren't posh enough in his estimation!

I dropped Robert back at his flat in Limehouse Causeway, fondly imagining that that was the end of the "Thalatta" affair. But I had quite underestimated the calibre of that particular child.

The following week George Jones came up to London to attend a meeting, and he dropped in to have a drink with us on his way back to Essex.

"That little Cockney sparrow you brought along to see us last week," he accosted me. "I suppose that you knew that he nearly caused us to miss the tide next morning, did you?"

"What on earth do you mean?" I replied defensively, with certain misgivings beginning to formulate in my mind.

"Well one of the girls happened to mention that we were due to leave at eight o'clock on Saturday morning, and just before eight he crept aboard, fairly exhausted after walking all the way from Limehouse," explained George. "Naturally we had to give him some breakfast after all that, and make it clear to him that he couldn't go to sea without his parents' consent. Then I sent the mate ashore with him to put him on the right bus for the return journey, so you can imagine what time we finally got under way!"

George took a long draught of bitter, then continued: "We've made Robert into our ship's mascot! He's just the sort of child we're trying so hard to buy another barge for. But the sad thing is that there will never be enough barges to accommodate all the thousands of little Cockney sparrows who have nowhere to go, and yet they're bursting with the spirit of adventure."

The Royal Naval College at Greenwich.

Chapter XIV

John's House

A tiny Indian child of exquisite beauty sauntered round to the entrance of the largest hut and engaged the old night-watchman in conversation. He was very fond of children so he chattered away happily to her for some minutes, little realizing that she had been sent as a decoy to distract his attention from what was happening elsewhere.

Suddenly a piercing whistle rent the air; an urgent warning that Mr Spence, the foreman, had just turned the corner of Brightlingsea Buildings. Four small urchins hurriedly emerged from an adjacent hut, each carrying some illicit articles of booty: one held a hack-saw, the second clutched a large hammer, the third had a pot of paint in one hand and a paraffin lamp in the other, and the last one was laden with a selection of useful household goods. They vanished as fast as their spindly little legs could carry them. All too late John, the night-watchman, noticed what had happened. A roar of impotent fury escaped from his lips as he shambled off across the wilderness of coarse grass and broken milk bottles in pursuit of the young robbers.

"Come back, ye divil's spawn!" he bellowed at the fast retreating boys. "Shure Oi'll be after bating the loife out o' ye one o' these days."

All over Brightlingsea Buildings and in the houses on the other side of the road curious spectators were craning their necks out of the windows, to see what the outcome of the nightly drama would be.

John had first arrived in the neighbourhood about the

same time as Murphy's gang started work on the sewers underneath Narrow Street. No one knew exactly where he had lived before or why he suddenly chose to come to Limehouse, but one afternoon he moved in and his presence was such that it was no easy feat to ignore him. All night long, and most of the day as well, he could be observed sitting inside his little shelter on the corner of the waste ground or lumbering up and down Ropemakers Fields, like some great Siberian bear finding its feet after the winter hibernation. He was a big man with a reddish face and small grey eyes which viewed the world suspiciously from under a pair of shaggy bristling eyebrows. He seldom washed or shaved, and he wore an odd assortment of clothes which helped to accentuate the impression that he had travelled a long distance from a land of wide open prairies, a far cry from the labyrinth of noisy dirty streets into which he had inadvertently wandered.

The poor man led a dreadful life to begin with, owing to the children who lived in the blocks of flats on either side of the waste ground. They tormented him unmercifully, and because he had arrived in the middle of the long

John and his little dog on the waste ground.

school holidays they hardly gave him a moment's peace. They used to climb up the wall on to the roof of his hut and batter holes in it from above: if he came outside to remonstrate with them, some particularly agile child would dart in through the entrance and steal anything within reach; but if he remained firmly entrenched inside his flimsy shelter, they would run off with some of the paraffin lamps which were intended to be placed each night around the craters caused by Murphy's excavations, and which the old man fussed over with the utmost diligence and care.

Despite all these aggravating set-backs, John seemed quite contented in his new surroundings and he soon made friends with a number of people who lived nearby. It was impossible to arrive by car in Ropemakers Fields at night, be it never so late, without the considerable figure of the night-watchman looming over one within a matter of seconds. Depending on whether it was a stranger or a friend who emerged from the car, he would appear intensely fierce and threatening or delightfully welcoming, with his soft Irish brogue. "Faith, if it isn't the gude doctor himself. And Oi was after wonderin' if the gintleman would be gracing this corner wid the light o' his presence? Its a heap o' throuble Oi've had tonight, Sorr, wid all those rampagin' divils up on the rufe again; but its meself that's a blathering fule not to liven up me ways an' catch the bhoys." After a while we began to watch the baiting of John from our kitchen window with a certain amount of anxiety, and when he disappeared for too long in pursuit of his tormentors we would take Texel for a stroll across the waste ground to make sure that he had not stumbled into one of the numerous muddy craters and sprained an ankle.

The long summer evenings imperceptibly grew shorter,

and suddenly one day all the drilling and tinkering in the Narrow Street drains was finished. Murphy's gang collected their tools and bits and pieces together, had a farewell drink with John in the Black Horse, and then a big lorry backed into Ropemakers Fields and spirited the men away to some remote sewers on the far side of London. All that remained was one forlorn little hut, sagging at the sides and open to the heavens by way of several grapefruit-sized holes in the roof.

That night John laid out a week's wages in pints of black and tan, for his job had come to an end and he had nothing in prospect for the morrow.

Just when it seemed that the future was very black indeed, a guardian angel must have looked down through the layers of dark clouds and perceived the poor night-watchman sitting in his flimsy hut, holding his aching head between two huge red paws. For the very next day his fortunes took a remarkable turn for the better.

During the course of the following morning an immense lorry, at least twice as large as the one which had removed Murphy's gang from the neighbourhood, drew up beneath the shadow of Limehouse Lil and disgorged a cheerful group of strangers, several of whom had flame-coloured hair and responded to the names of Dick, Paddy, Danny and Terry. The first thing they did on alighting from their lorry was to set up a colossal notice-board on the corner of the waste ground, just at the point where Ropemakers Fields runs into Narrow Street. It announced that J. B. Riney and Co. were about to widen the road, and they wished to apologise for any inconvenience they might cause people in the process. Having firmly secured this proclamation to the rugged soil of Limehouse, they repaired to the Black Horse to quench their not inconsiderable thirsts.

Riney's gang re-appeared about the middle of the afternoon, arm in arm with their fellow-countryman, John, and they gave a powerful rendering of "The Mountains of Mourne" as they strolled back to their lorry and started to unload it. And that was the precise moment when some magic agency appears to have been at work on behalf of the night-watchman.

The lorry disgorged a few score wooden planks, several small window and door frames, three tiny roofs in collapsible sections, large sheets of corrugated iron and boxes of assorted nails and screws, as well as an enormous hamper of tools.

Inspired by their refreshment in the Black Horse, Riney's gang set to work in an energetic manner. All afternoon the sound of sawing, chiselling, hammering, singing, screwing and more hammering rent the still

Rebuilding the south side of Limehouse Basin.

summer air; and before the sun had set behind Tower Bridge that evening there were three little houses nestling snugly within a corrugated iron enclosure, set in the apex of the triangle formed by the portion of the waste ground which lay between our house and Ropemakers Fields. That waste ground, which belonged to no one and to everyone, was one of the strangest features of the Limehouse landscape. It sprouted miniature hills and giant craters, abandoned three-piece suites, retired perambulators and prehistoric motor cars; and in amongst them all the sturdy London flowers took seed and flourished exuberantly.

The morning after the arrival of the three houses, Riney's cheerful gang backed their lorry into Ropemakers Fields once again, and this time it was filled with an assorted cargo of household goods, the sight of which caused the night-watchman's eyes to grow round and deeply thoughtful. I saw a bed, two tables, numerous chairs, a stove, a kettle and mugs, kitchen utensils and boxes filled with groceries being unloaded and taken into the largest of the three huts; then came some rather smart chintz curtains, a few electrical fittings, brooms, scrubbers, buckets, floor cloths, bedding and a hundred and one oddments which all add to the comfort of a civilized home.

It took three days before the tiny hamlet on the waste ground was completed, for as well as the furnishing and decoration of the inside of the huts, their outer walls were enlivened with a couple of coats of pale grey paint. During this exciting interlude John circled round and round those stupendous erections, admiring them from all angles and complimenting the builders on their skill in the most flattering Irish fashion:

"It's a hypocrite ye moight be after callin' me for mintioning the fact, but niver in all me loife have Oi sane sich a foine group o' dwillings. Shure its only an Oirishman would know how to raise sich bewtiful architicture!"

On the fourth morning the yellow monsters arrived. They were huge and splendid vehicles intended for crushing, mixing and bulldozing the historic soil of Limehouse into a state of uniform submission, and for smoothing out the wrinkled surface of the landscape so that it would be fit to build a road across. The big monsters had attendant baby monsters known as dumper-trucks, and there was even a mobile yellow crane which provoked enormous pleasure amongst the children of the neighbourhood.

Mr Spence, the foreman, arrived simultaneously. He was a good-looking middle-aged Irishman who controlled his team of workmen in the most admirable way. His first appearance in Narrow Street was closely observed by a group of discriminating housewives, their heads festooned with steel curlers; "Ain't 'e gorjus!" one of them exclaimed. "'Ope they'll keep my ole man locked up while 'e's arahnd'.

It was not long before the question of John was brought to his attention. The site was badly in need of a reliable night-watchman with so much valuable machinery lying about, and the old man had done his utmost to persuade the boys to put in a good word for him. After due consideration Mr Spence agreed to take him on, and that same evening he moved out of his miserable little shelter into the palatial quarters provided by J.B. Riney and Co. He was to live in the largest of the three huts, and it did not take him long to unpack his few possessions and make himself thoroughly at home there.

For the next few months John lived in the seventh heaven, and his life took on an entirely new complexion. Perhaps it was because he felt so happy and secure that the children gradually stopped aggravating him, and many of them became his devoted friends. Part of his week's wages were always spent on sweets and chocolates for them, and he often gave their mothers extra money to buy them special treats. His tormentors seemed to have evaporated into thin air, and in their place a group of boys and girls with the innocent faces of cherubs would cluster round the door of his hut every day, run errands for him, help place his paraffin lamps in position in the evenings and keep him company on all occasions, except when he was celebrating his good fortune in the Black Horse.

The Queen's Silver Jubilee occurred about that time, and the inhabitants of Brightlingsea Buildings celebrated it with a fancy-dress party and a splendid feast in the open courtyard behind the flats. Our Indian friends, Lal Singh and his family, appeared in their finest costumes, and there were various neighbours from our side of Narrow Street such as David Owen and Janet Street-Porter who judged the fancy-dress competition; and John climbed up on to a wooden platform in a corner of the courtyard and sang the most beautiful Irish songs

John Sharkey singing "Danny Boy" outside Faraday Dwellings.

which brought tears to the eyes of many of his audience.

That autumn the days drifted by in a golden haze, each one more glorious than the last. For two months not a drop of rain descended on the dusty streets of Limehouse and never a cloud obscured the pale orange face of the sun. Early each morning the yellow monsters went to work, and snatches of Irish folk-songs drifted up through our kitchen windows whilst we were eating our breakfast. And before very long the whole appearance of Narrow Street and the adjoining waste ground began to alter.

When we had first come to live there it was still a very slender alley with an old iron bollard on the corner of Ropemakers Fields, which was placed there originally to prevent the horse-drawn vehicles from rubbing up against the fronts of the houses. Also there was a prominent bulge in the road opposite Duncan Dunbar's warehouses which made it even narrower than before at the point where it swung round a sharp bend. There were no pavements worth mentioning, and the heavy lorries used to thunder past our

Janet Street-Porter with some of the prize winners and Michael Collins dressed as a social worker!

Some children from Brightlingsea Buildings in fancy-dress for the Queen's Silver Jubilee.

house at such a speed that the whole building trembled from time to time, and pedestrians had to flatten themselves against the walls to stay alive.

By the middle of November Riney's men had accomplished the most amazing transformation. Suddenly Narrow Street was no longer narrow, and the places where two horses would have been hard pressed to pass each other without rubbing flanks had grown wide enough to allow a couple of the largest lorries to pass each other in comfort. Also there were no more sharp bends to negotiate, just a few gentle curves with a fine white pavement bordering them on either side.

Simultaneously the yellow monsters turned their attention to the waste ground, and it was not long before they had reduced that wild jungle landscape into a neat brown prairie which resembled a ploughed field. Dick was strolling across it with Texel one evening when he found a curious reddish-yellow object on a pile of freshly turned rubble, which he thought might be a fossilized human bone. I took it to the Natural History Museum next day and was told that it was the skeletal remains of a sponge of the Upper Chalk Period, which was about a hundred million years ago.

John was becoming very domesticated in his new home, and he had been given a small black and tan bitch to keep him company. She had soft silky fur and tragic brown eyes, and she was very fastidious about her food so her master would often spend substantial sums of money at the butcher's, buying her special cuts of steak or lamb. He fixed up a kennel adjoining his hut, and a swarm of children used to gather round it when school was over, to play with the little bitch and talk to the night-watchman.

Every night when darkness fell, John never failed to surround Dick's car with a positive necklace of glowing red paraffin lamps. Coinciding with us in the parking-bay on one of these occasions, he complained that his feet were hurting him so badly that he could hardly walk any more, so Dick gave him an old pair of soft suede shoes which had come from Simpson's and were known as 'cruise shoes'.

They fitted him perfectly and were exceptionally comfortable, he declared. A few days later there was a torrential rainstorm and the waste ground turned into a glutinous quagmire. We were

John's house, my car and the widening of Narrow Street.

looking out of our kitchen window that evening when we saw the unusual sight of Simpson's cruise shoes, thickly coated in brown mud and fresh tar, making their way along Ropemakers Fields in the direction of the Black Horse!

Towards the end of November the dark clouds began to gather on John's horizon once again, and we found him waiting outside our door one night on our return from a dinner-party. The poor man appeared to be in a very unhappy state of mind, and he told Dick that he wanted a private word with him about an extremely important matter. It appeared that Mr Spence had told the boys that the job in Limehouse would be finished by Christmastime, and they would then be moving on to a new road-widening scheme in the Borough of Hackney. Nothing had been said to John directly, but he surmised that his domesticated bliss might come to an abrupt end in a few week's time, and he could perceive no gleams of light at all in the future which lay ahead of him.

That night he told Dick something of his life-story. He had been born in Roscommon and went to a school for simple children, as he put it, until he was fourteen. After that he became a tramp and had spent most of his life wandering up and down the roads of Great Britain until, one day, he came to Limehouse... And this was the first proper home he'd ever had, he told Dick with a tremulous note in his voice and a sweeping gesture of the hands towards his domain which might have described a baronial hall surrounded by acres of parkland, instead of a little wooden hut set in a sea of mud.

The outcome of the conversation was that Dick promised to have a word with Mr Spence about the chances of taking John along with them to their new site in Hackney. His house would certainly be moving on there, so it seemed reasonable to us that he should be allowed to accompany it.

Mr Spence suffered from asthma during the cold misty mornings of late autumn, and he sometimes felt inclined to discuss his symptoms with Dick if they met by chance in Narrow Street. One such occasion occurred shortly after John's appeal, so he listened sympathetically to the foreman's wheezing voice for some minutes, before sounding him very delicately on the subject of the night-watchman. Well aware that it was absolutely none of our business, Dick somehow contrived to handle the conversation in such a way that Mr Spence ended up by thinking that he himself had first conceived the idea of taking John along with them to Hackney, and Dick was the one who congratulated him on his humane proposals. However, nothing conclusive was settled at that first conference, although the prospects did not seem entirely unfavourable. Mr Spence told Dick that he would have to ask the permission of the boss before deciding, and if John came with them he could not bring Susie to the new site, as the hut would be in the middle of a road with no facilities for keeping a dog there.

As soon as the foreman was out of sight, we sought out John to tell him the verdict. He seemed satisfied on the whole, although rather upset about his dog of whom he had grown very fond. We promised to try and find a good home for her if he was allowed to remain with Riney's firm.

There were no further developments during the next two weeks until Johnny Roberts, the little boy from Brightlingsea Buildings with one arm disabled by polio, came round one morning to tell me that the old man had been taken to hospital to have an operation.

'They took 'im orff in a nambulance rahnd 'arf eight," he announced, with his anxious brown eyes as round as ping-pong balls. "An' when I come dahn te 'elp 'im fetch in 'is lamps, 'e wasn't there no more so poor ole Susie ain't 'alf creatin', an' she won't even drink 'er milk what I brought dahn fer er."

He started snivelling into a dirty old handkerchief and his little sister, Vera, came running across the road to comfort him. Some of Riney's men confirmed this story, and they told me that John had an ulcer which was playing him up very badly, but no one seemed to know which hospital he had been taken to.

Meanwhile Mrs Collins, a young Irish widow living in Brightlingsea Buildings, whose children had been amongst John's most devoted friends, took Susie up to her flat to look after her; and when the school closed that afternoon a forlorn little crowd stood around aimlessly on the corner of the waste ground, staring fixedly at John's house as if they thought that the harder they stared at his door the more likely he was to appear framed in the entrance, come what may.

Dick sought out Mr Spence that evening, and he promised to find out what had become of the old man as we wanted to visit him after his operation. We waited anxiously for news, and early next morning the foreman came round to share with us the dramatic sequel to John's disappearance. He had been put in a ward on the ground floor of the Poplar Hospital to await his operation, and as soon as the Sister's back was turned he climbed out through a window and shambled all the way back to Limehouse under cover of darkness. Mr Spence went on to say that he was now back in his hut with the door locked and bolted from the inside, as he was so afraid of someone coming to take him back to the hospital, and also of the possibility of losing his home if he was absent for a few days.

This state of affairs continued for two days, and no one caught a glimpse of John, nor were Riney's men able to brew their morning tea on the stove as the hut appeared utterly impregnable, like a fortress prepared to withstand a lengthy siege. The foreman nevertheless happened to know that the old man had hardly any food in his larder, as he had always spent most of his wages the same day that he received them on drinks for his friends, sweets for the children and special titbits for Susie.

By the third afternoon we all became anxious for his welfare, so I collected a parcel of nourishing food for him and Dick took it across to the hut on his return from work. He knocked loudly several times but not a mouse stirred inside, so he called to John through the keyhole and asked

John Sharkey in the middle of the much wider Narrow Street.

him to open the door. He was answered by a fierce growl on the other side of the wooden partition, and a bearlike voice enunciated the two words "fuck off", quite distinctly. Discouraged by this reception, he put the parcel on the ground outside the door and went away.

Later that evening one of Riney's men thought of a more subtle way of extracting the night-watchman from his hut. He ordered a pint of John's favourite beer in the Black Horse, then walked across to the hut and whispered through the keyhole that he wanted to treat his old friend to a pint of black and tan, and it was at that very moment waiting for him on the counter of the public bar. This was more than the old man could resist; a few seconds later he emerged from his lair, looking more like a bear than ever, and casting a suspicious glance around the neighbourhood he hurried across the road and into the pub.

Paddy, who had lured him out by this gambit, bought John more than one pint and when he was showing signs of approaching mellowness, left him for a few minutes to remove both the key and the bolts from the inside of the hut. Later that night John agreed to go back to his home if Paddy would promise to lock him in personally, and never allow the key to stray into anyone else's hands.

For the next week or so the neighbours and Riney's men made it their business to look after John, and to bring him plenty of food. Gradually he regained his strength and no further mention was made of his ulcer.

The next time the old man saw Dick he was overcome with embarrassment, and implored forgiveness for what he had said inside his hut that evening:

"Faith and Oi was after thinkin' ye moight be one o'

those doctors from the hospital who was wantin' to fitch me back!" he explained. "If Oi'd known it was his self from across the road, Oi'd niver have said sich a tirrible word, be Jasus Oi wouldn't!"

Shortly after his illness John suddenly transferred his patronage to The Grapes, after a somewhat obscure tiff in the Black Horse during which he was reputed to have used an insulting expression to the landlady. He invited us to take a farewell drink with him one evening, and he told us rather sadly that he would be leaving in a few days time as Mr Spence had at last confirmed that he could continue his job with Riney's gang. He asked me to print our name, address and telephone number very clearly on a piece of paper so that he could get in touch with us whenever he felt like doing so.

The end came very fast indeed. Early one morning in mid-December Mr Spence announced that his gang were to move on to Hackney the following afternoon, and John came shuffling across the road to leave Susie with us as we had found a home for her in the Essex countryside.

A few hours later he left Narrow Street in the back of an open lorry which contained the walls and roof of his house, as well as the door and window frames. Two of the most magnificent of the yellow monsters acted as his escort, one as the vanguard whilst the other protected his rear.

Three days before Christmas there was a brief but heavy snowfall over Limehouse, which obliterated the last signs of the little hamlet which had stood for so many months on the corner of the waste ground. The neighbourhood lay subdued and silent under a pure white mantle of ice crystals, only disturbed, here and there, by small footprints criss-crossing the empty landscape.

Chapter XV

The Christmas Party

The olive-green sky merged imperceptibly with the olive-green river, a weird oppressive wall of greenness which seemed to grip the entire expanse of Limehouse Reach within its stifling embrace. Then the snow came; just a few soft white flakes to begin with, but soon the whole atmosphere was alive with minute particles of virgin ice, those ethereal crystalline droplets which come floating down from heaven with a gentle sigh of pleasure to announce their arrival on the solid surface of our planet.

I always feel a peculiar tingling sensation in my veins when the first snow comes, an inkling of enormous primeval excitement such as the natives of Greenland or Northern Siberia must experience at the end of the brief hot summer. On that particular morning, with the spirit of Christmas hovering about in the air, I flattened my nose against the window-pane and began to daydream about a long journey I was making across the tundra in a sleigh drawn by six reindeer.

"You'd soon get bored in your sleigh," observed Dick, who is never slow at reading my thoughts. "And you'd have frozen fingers and toes and possibly a frost-bitten nose, and nothing but a few polar bears to keep you company!"

"Just look at the barges with their glistening white decks," I replied contentedly, pointing out of the window at "Mullet" and "Stickleback" and completely ignoring his last remarks. "And there's an apricot patch in the sky

above Lavender Pond with a marvellous shaft of sunlight just about to break through it. Do come and see!"

We stood by the window watching the snow falling and the pale winter sun penetrating that iridescent curtain. Down below on the balcony our two little fir trees were clad in shining white bonnets, and out on the river beyond them a grey phantom ship stole silently downstream on the ebb.

"What a perfect setting for our party," I murmured to myself, almost inaudibly.

"Not EVERYone enjoys wading around the streets ankle-deep in wet slush," retorted my husband. "And, moreover, we may find that half of them won't turn up at all," he added hopefully.

Any further discussion on the prevailing weather was curtailed by the sound of the front door bell ringing, loud and clear. If you live in a tall thin house with a steep staircase in the East End, you seldom descend to the ground floor to answer a summons to the front door, unless you are expecting company. "You'd be up an' dahn the fuckin' stairs all day long, like a fuckin' yo-yo !" as one of our neighbours from the buildings across the road put it most concisely. This being a proven fact, Dick went down to the kitchen on the second floor, threw up one of the windows, extended his neck well out beyond the window-ledge and demanded to know the business

Above: Our Christmas tree.

of the two small figures peering through our letter-box at street level.

It turned out to be Johnny and Vera from Brightlingsea Buildings, and as it was Saturday morning and they were not in school, they had come across to see if they could run any errands for us. Dick did some quick thinking then asked the children to fetch an extra pint of milk from Bernie's, the little grocer's shop in Three Colts Street.

"What sort o milk?" bawled Johnny, who knew perfectly well but wanted to prolong the conversation by any means in his power. "Cow's milk!" thundered Dick, with great presence of mind. We had been caught that way before, thinking they meant red or gold-topped bottles, and not appreciating the horror with which many East End families still regard genuine unadulterated cow's milk, that sinister white liquid which was said to harbour the tuberculosis bacteria in olden days.

We watched the children running down the street, Johnny with his limp right arm, the result of polio, dangling out of his old black duffel-coat, and Vera pelting him with snowballs filled with mud whilst she fed him noisy vocal titbits in her deep gruff voice. She was a small eight-year-old girl with clear innocent-looking eyes, and there was something completely incongruous about that extraordinary voice of hers.

The previous week Johnny and Vera's parents had received an unexpected bit of good news. On the day of its arrival the children ran across the street and battered on our door more urgently than usual. A moment later they burst into the hall, each one anxious to be the first

to announce their portentous tidings. By holding one grubby hand firmly across Vera's mouth, Johnny was able to get his say in first .... "We're goin' te be re'oused in Danegam just arter Christmas," he roared at me; "in a real 'ouse wiv a garden back'n'front!"

My first reaction was to wonder why anyone should feel so excited about leaving Limehouse; then I remembered that Johnny's father was an old-age pensioner and their mother had to stay at home to look after him, and five of them lived in a poky little flat across the road which would certainly not compare favourably with a house and garden of their own. By this time Vera had broken away from her brother's restraining arm and was able to supplement the news with many colourful details about their new home. I gathered that they were moving to Dagenham, the Mecca of all the East Enders who feel the urge to leave their old surroundings for the better life. Their big brother, Peter, had already taken a day off from work and gone there to inspect the house and neighbourhood, and his report was entirely favourable. The family were due to leave Brightlingsea Buildings early in the New Year, and although the children could

Above: Vera and Johnny Roberts in Regent's Park.

194

be a perfect pest on occasions, the idea of them disappearing to the wilds of Essex suddenly seemed rather sad.

On the morning of our party the genuine cow's milk arrived in due course and after the children had gone, Dick and I set to work on the final preparations for that evening. The party was to be held in Trevor's pad, it being the largest room in our house, and already we had spent several hours decorating the Christmas tree which stood on a wooden bench in front of the window, adorning the room with lanterns and streamers, holly and mistletoe, and arranging our Christmas cards on lengths of string which were suspended from the old oak beams across the ceiling.

Earlier that week Jimmy Jones and Billy Taxi had helped Dick to carry a barrel of bitter round from The Grapes. After its arrival there had been all the rigmarole of 'racking' it, which means arranging the barrel at a suitable angle on its stand so that the beer will soon settle down after its recent journey; and 'tapping' it, the thrilling moment when the tap is hammered home and the very first drops of beer are drawn from it into a half-pint tankard and sampled with the appropriate solemnity it demands.

It was now Saturday, December 19th, the prelude to the winter season and the morning of the day when our party was due to take place, and we were both filled with a fervent desire to cancel the whole wretched affair! As this was not possible, we walked to Salmon Lane with Texel and bought huge quantities of bread, butter, cheese, ham, pickled onions and pickled gherkins. Then we came back across the sparkling white churchyard and threw snowballs at each other and our dog. After that we felt better, and on reaching home Dick drew two glasses of bitter from our private barrel and we drank them in front of the Christmas tree before settling down to cut a huge mountain of sandwiches in the kitchen.

The previous year I had made the fatal mistake of serving a number of delicacies such as lobster vol-au-vents, quiche Lorraine and spiced chicken in aspic. These were regarded with the deepest suspicion by most of our guests; in fact a dish of poisoned toadstools could hardly have received a worse reception. That being the case, I determined to play safe at our next party and my one and only concession to the Christmas spirit was a tray of mince-pies, without which I would have felt that the party was sadly lacking.

The day wore slowly on, and because I am nearly always late Dick insisted on my going upstairs to change at least an hour before the party was due to start. Meanwhile he went out to buy a bottle of orange squash, a last minute thought in case any of our guests should happen to prefer a soft drink.

I had just reached that state of undress when it takes several minutes either to retreat into what one has recently thrown off or advance into the fresh garments one intends to put on, when the front door bell rang; well, it didn't just ring in the ordinary sense of the word, but it continued to ring on one long high-pitched note, incessantly, maddeningly and quite unforgivably early, if it was really our first guest arriving! In my haste to stop that excruciating din I threw on some clothes, half of one sort and half of the other, and hurried down the stairs, two at a time, quite forgetting our usual practice of looking out of the kitchen window first. At last I reached the front door and flung one half of it open, it being the type which opens down the middle; and there was Vera hanging like a small chimpanzee from our door-knocker, with her right fist pressed hard up against the bell. Her feet were about eighteen inches off the ground, and as soon as she saw me she smiled ecstatically and shouted, "See! I've found a way te reach your bell at last. Johnny lifted me up so as I could 'ang on te the knocker an' git me other 'and up on te the bell!"

I felt completely at a loss for words as I considered the various aspects of the situation. There was I, desperately trying to get ready for that gruesome bout of revelry we had let ourselves in for in a moment of sheer insanity, and there was Vera, quite oblivious to my unhappy predicament, suspended from our door-knocker with an expression of exquisite enjoyment and achievement lighting up her grey-

"Britannia" speeding upriver with a Sun tug in attendance.

green eyes. I grabbed hold of her round the waist and prized her fingers away from both the knocker and the bell, then deposited her firmly on the pavement and held her there to ensure a few seconds of peace and quiet. Then Peter appeared, like an angel from heaven, to fetch his little sister home; and, simultaneously, Dick returned with the orange squash.

There were no further interruptions during the next forty-five minutes and, much to my surprise, we both found ourselves dressed and ready, with all the candles lit in the hall and Trevor's pad and enough time in hand for me to suffer acutely from that sinking sensation which always precedes any form of entertainment personally arranged by us.

The front door bell rang once more. This time it was a short crisp note which put me into a fresh dither. Dick went to open it and ushered in our first guest, Miss Edith Ramsey, M.B.E., one of those rare phenomena, a legendary figure who was still alive. She had lived and worked in the East End for more than half a century, and in her opinion there was no place on earth more beautiful or desirable than Whitechapel.

The next people to arrive were our old friends Brian and Pat Bland from Blackheath, closely followed by Jack and Renie from The Grapes, the rector, Mr Watts, and his wife and son, and John Doble, the young man from the Foreign Office who went to work by dinghy every morning if the tide was suitable.

The party was slowly but surely getting under way. Not very gay to begin with, after the manner of most parties, but the first pints of bitter were being sampled judiciously by those who suspected that there might be a long evening ahead of them, and the conversation was exploratory and a trifle constrained.

The next time the door-bell rang it was the Wapping contingent who came in out of the snowy night, all eleven of them bearing gramophone records and sparkling Christmas parcels in their arms. There were old Lucy Durrell's two daughters, Minnie and Cissie, Minnie's husband and brother-in-law, Johnny and Lenny, and her daughter and son-in-law, Junie and Tommy, and Cissie's lifelong friend, Anna; then there were Minnie's two nieces, Marie and Ada, and Ada had brought her husband and one of her daughters. Marie, who had just left school, and was looking very glamorous in a black and white horizontally striped blouse, black velvet hot-pants, black shoes and stockings and long matching eye-lashes.

As soon as Wapping had disrobed itself and paid a visit to the bathroom, the party moved into phase two. Marie took charge of the record-player and put on an old favourite called "Party-time at the Astor", a medley of all the best known Cockney songs; meanwhile the rest of her family took over the far end of the room, the river end so to speak, where all the women were able to find seats close to the Christmas tree and where Miss Ramsay soon joined them to chat about Wapping in the old days. The barrel of beer was working non-stop by then, and Dick was kept hard at work filling glasses whilst Pat and I passed round the sandwiches, cheese cubes, etc.

After Wapping, the long distance guests began to arrive. Dick's brother and sister-in-law, Anthony and Jenny, and my two oldest friends, Sue and Winkle. It was the same Sue who had gone exploring with me in

Wapping and Limehouse all those years ago, when we had first met Lucy Durrell and her husband in the Prospect of Whitby; and the same Winkle whose owl accompanied us down the river on our adventurous voyage to Southend and back.

Suddenly a ship with a deep-throated siren called out to us from the other side of the windows, only a stone's throw away in Limehouse Reach, and the passage of time was swept away in the secure knowledge that nothing would change in a thousand years out on that old grey river. Simultaneously it ushered in Mike Uglow, who had just left the R.A.F. to become a doctor in the Essex Health Department. Marie had increased the volume of sound on the record-player to full blast and, encouraged by this deafening uproar, half the room had begun to dance. The constrained atmosphere which I had noticed earlier was rapidly being replaced by a cheerful buzz of conversation, snatches of song, clapping of hands and stamping of feet in rhythm with the music, and the steady flow of bitter from the barrel to the glass. I

Above: Winkle and Sue having lunch at the Prospect of Whitby.

breathed a sigh of relief, and my own private sinking sensation began to diminish.

"They must all be here by now," Dick whispered to me as we watched the joyful prancing throng in the middle of Trevor's pad. "Not likely!" answered the door-knocker, interpreting our thoughts. And two minutes later the rest of the Limehouse contingent were jostling each other in the narrow hall. There was Lou and Bert from Brightlingsea Buildings across the road; he worked at West Ham Technical College and was an artist of no mean ability in his spare time; and his wife, a woman of splendid proportions with a heart of gold and a remarkable strength of character which was nurtured in the tough old days on the Isle of Dogs, when her father was a docker with thirteen children to bring up. Besides Lou and Bert, there was Jimmy Jones and his wife, Frances; Keith, the foreman of the Stepney Power Station, and his wife, Grace; David Livermore, the boy with the long brown hair and liquid brown eyes from the barge yard; Marcus and Jessica Morris, our charming neighbours from Number 82; and, last of all, our old friend from The Grapes, Billy Taxi, and his pretty wife and daughter, Alice and Tina. Gradually the new arrivals were assimilated into the party and I ran upstairs to fetch another mound of sandwiches, muttering to myself with satisfaction; "That really IS the last guest!"

After a head-on collision with Cissie, who was just emerging from the bathroom, I had started up the second flight of stairs when the bell rang once more, an unusually resonant and imperious summons it seemed to me. I knew that Dick must be hard at work with the beer barrel just then, so 1 turned tail and sprinted back down the stairs, this time almost annihilating Lenny who was next in line for the bathroom.

"Who on earth can it possibly be?" I asked myself, having just finished a rapid mental calculation of all those who had entered our house during the past two hours. Texel, who is no great lover of parties, barked in sympathy with me as she pushed past me down the staircase. I was quite out of breath by the time I reached the hall, and my best party shoes were beginning to pinch my toes. I opened the door cautiously and lo and behold, there was old Dan waiting in the snow outside! Dan from Bugsby's Hole, who had been so reluctant to decide one way or the other about our invitation, and there he was dressed in a smart grey suit with a collar and tie, and a sapphire-blue waistcoat which exactly matched the colour of his seafaring eyes. Dick had come out into the hall by this time, and he was no less surprised than I had been to see Dan at our Christmas party.

"Thought I'd drop in fer a few minutes as I just 'appened to be passin' through Li'mus," observed the old sailor defensively, as we led him towards Trevor's pad.

At that moment the room was undergoing a brief interval of comparative peace in between "Any Old Iron" and "Down at the Old Bull and Bush". Dan surveyed the whole scene with extreme apprehension, and for one moment I thought he was going to turn round and escape through the front door before it was too late and his retreat was cut off; then, as if by divine intervention, he spotted someone on the far side of the room in the Wapping encampment who caught his particular attention.

"Funny thing!" the old man remarked to Dick, rubbing his eyes with a gnarled fist. "I s'pose me old eyes must be deceivin' me; but there's a woman over there what looks the spittin' image of a doll I went te school wiv, gone sixty years or more!"

"How extraordinary," replied my husband, giving me a significant flicker of the left eyelid behind Dan's back. "Well, come across and meet our friends from Wapping and perhaps you might find someone you know amongst them."

Dick and Dan steered an intricate course across the room, and when they reached the far side the old man made straight for one corner of our big green sofa where Anna was sitting quietly beside her old friend, Cissie. The moment she noticed Dan her kindly pink face expressed a series of fleeting emotions; bewilderment, reminiscence, the dawning of recognition, then delight swept over it in quick succession, like fast-moving clouds crossing the face of the sun. By the time he had thumped her on the back with a large brown paw, there was no doubt left in our minds that Anna was the doll who went to school with Dan in Wapping, way back in the early years of that century.

By that time the party had moved into its third phase, what you might describe as the uninhibited peak of the whole affair. The barrel, which no longer required three strong men to move it on its rack, had done its work after the fashion of all good wooden casks which are specially designed to house some potent liquid. The barriers of shyness and reserve had quite dissolved, and the gulf between Wapping and Limehouse had been spanned by a slender bridge. In fact everyone was dancing, singing, laughing and drinking together, and one or two people gradually began to distinguish themselves in the same way that a sky full of stars will usually provide an occasional orb that shines more brilliantly than all its neighbours.

Keith, who had greeted Miss Ramsay like a long-lost friend, suddenly took up an arresting stance in the middle of the room and began to sing a song entitled; "God bless the Barley Mow". At any time of day Keith is a commanding figure of a man, and that particular evening he looked quite magnificent with his immense brown beard surmounting a claret-coloured bow-tie, and a pint tankard in his right hand with which he emphasised the salient points in his ditty. It was followed by thunderous applause, so Keith seesawed from one foot to the other under the red paper lantern, cleared his throat for further action and gave the assembled company a full-blooded but somewhat unusual interpretation of an old West Country folk-song. By the time he had reached the fourth verse, Dick, who is faster than anyone else I know at sensing an atmosphere, had detected a slight bleakness in the eyes of one or two ladies present. Being a man of resource and not wishing to offend Keith, he quickly made his dispositions and by the time the old English folk-song was drawing to an uproarious finish, he was already leading Dr Mike Uglow towards the piano and demanding silence for our next guest artiste.

Mike was a very shy and sensitive person, as well as

being a great lover of music and a pianist of the first order. But he was not overjoyed when he suddenly found himself the centre of attention, the focal point in the room on to whom every eye was trained. However, even the worst moments in life do not linger forever, and the brave pianist had soon forgotten his unhappy plight as the music from his finger-tips soared joyfully up through the smoke-laden air. Many of those who were aesthetically inclined clustered around the piano, whilst another group of a more down-to-earth genre began to form at the far end of the room.

After a few minutes of sheer delight I ran upstairs to the kitchen to fetch a dish of pickled gherkins, and when I returned to the ground floor an extraordinary sound greeted my ears. Mike was playing "Silent Night" very delicately on the piano and Cissie was giving a powerful rendering of "Any Time", her favourite song, in the centre of the other group near the Christmas tree!

A few minutes later the record-player was going full blast once more, and Winkle leapt on to the floor and did a solo dance of the languishing gipsy variety; she was soon joined by Johnny who became a wandering apache in search of a gipsy, and as it developed in momentum and originality a circle began to form round the two performers, stamping its feet and clapping its hands in rhythm with the dance.

Minnie was undoubtedly the queen of the ball during the third phase of the party. It was a splendid sight to watch her leading her particular group in "Knees up Mother Brown", her copper-red hair flashing in the candle-light, her face beaming like an oriental sunrise and her knees going up and down with the speed of pistons in an internal combustion chamber. She sang lustily all the time that she danced, and as I watched her I felt quite nostalgic for the days of long ago when her mother used to lead that merry prancing circle in the public bar of the Prospect of Whitby.

The clock began to chime twelve times for midnight and, simultaneously, the room was plunged into darkness and the music ceased. Everyone turned towards the door where a faint glimmer of light surrounded by dancing black shadows grew in intensity from one second to the next. And suddenly Father Christmas was framed in the door-way, a heavy sack slung over his left shoulder and a flickering candle held in his right hand. His shaggy eyebrows and long white beard were encrusted with frozen snow, and he gave Dick some crisp instructions about the tethering of his reindeer to a nearby lamp-post, before advancing into the centre of the room.

Texel barked fiercely from a safe distance whilst Father Christmas opened his sack and began to rummage inside it. He drew out two or three dozen parcels with small labels attached to them, and as he read out the name on each label in turn, it was claimed by a dim figure from the shadows outside the circle of radiance evoked by his candle. But anyone who was watching those proceedings very closely might have noticed that Tina, the charming little daughter of Billy Taxi, came out into the candle-light on two occasions; first to receive a parcel for herself, but later on to claim a second one on behalf of her father!

As soon as everyone in the room had been catered for

by the magic sack, the old man bid them all a merry Christmas and stole out into the wintry night to look for his reindeer. The lights came on again and Keith started to draw the corks in a number of bottles of home-made wine which he had brought as a present for us. Whilst he and Dick were pouring it into some small glasses, Pat and I ran upstairs to fetch the mince-pies which I had put in the oven to keep warm. When we returned to the ground floor the party had already moved into phase four, or the final phase. Mike was playing Christmas carols very softly on the piano and before long everyone was drinking Keith's wine, eating mince-pies and wishing one another all the old traditional Christmas wishes. The lights on the Christmas tree were reflected in the dark window-panes behind them and the port and starboard lights of a tug suddenly mingled with that multi-coloured glow, a brief reunion before they sped away into the night on their voyage to London Town. Then Mother Thames's barges came together with a mighty clang, to let us know for certain that a ship had passed our house.

I rubbed my eyes to see if I was dreaming, for the serene bewitchment of phase four seemed such an amazing contrast to the previous noisy rumpus. We had not planned that sudden transition ourselves, so it must have been the Christmas angel on the top of our tree, waving her magic wand over the old house by the river.

Some while later the long distance guests began to leave. Parcels inscribed "Do not open till December 25th", Christmas greetings and powerful hugs were exchanged, and slowly they drifted away, two by two. Then Minnie decided that it was time for her family to go home, so Dick and I set off with two full car-loads towards Wapping.

I felt quite intoxicated by my immediate surroundings as the car took charge and seemed to fly through the night sky like Father Christmas's sleigh. The air was made of vintage champagne and the streets were strewn with sparkling diamonds; the two old lamps on the hump-backed bridge across Limehouse Cut cast fitful shadows on the walls of the dark warehouses, and a slender funnel between two masts, the tallest of which sprouted a glowing Christmas tree from its summit, moved swiftly downstream past the narrow entrance to the Cut. Minnie, who was wedged between Anna and the gear lever, suddenly burst into song ....

"Maybe its because I'm a Londoner,

That I love London Town... " she boomed.

"Maybe its because I'm a Londoner,

That I think of her wherever I go;" rejoiced Cissie from the back seat.

"I get a funny feeling inside o' me,

Just walkin' up and down,

Maybe its because I'm a Londoner,

That I love London Town..."

roared the whole car-load, as we came to a grinding halt outside Riverside Mansions.

The Wapping contingent disembarked and we took to the night sky again and flew east, leaving eleven little figures huddled inside Sunday-best coats waving goodbye under a lamp-post in Monza Street.

Back in Limehouse the snow crystals crunched defiantly underfoot and up above us the dark blue velvet sky was encrusted with a million stars; bigger and more brilliant stars than you can see on any ordinary night in the year. And the proud black figure of Limehouse Lil rose triumphantly in their midst, a warm-hearted goddess shedding black soot over the pure white city beneath her.

As we turned to go indoors Dick murmured softly; "I really believe there IS some magic left in this world."

*   *   *

Chapter XVI

Vibrant Narrow Street
Leading To Celestial Canary Wharf

Limehouse Lil was the first of our old friends to go. One morning she was standing there with curly black whirls of smoke rising happily above the roof-tops into a cloudless blue sky; and the next morning a team of ruthless men were busy hacking away at her long slim body, covering the ground where she stood with smoky smashed-up bricks. "Have you heard about the exciting new marina they're going to build here instead of that monstrosity?" gushed one of our new neighbours, a "Yuppee" who had recently moved into Narrow Street.

I stepped quickly to one side as I felt tears creeping down my cheeks. After Limehouse Lil, there was one sadness after another. I do not remember in which order they followed each other, but the Limehouse landscape soon began to change out of all recognition; it was no longer a scruffy district of the bombed-out East End but, according to the large display boards erected by well-known Estate Agents, it was fast becoming "Fashionable Limehouse Village" filled with luxury apartments which had stunning river views, many of them located in vibrant Narrow Street.

The Regent Canal Dock sprouted numerous pontoons for yachts and canal-barges, surrounded by tall blocks of expensive flats, a picturesque harbour-master's office and a smart yacht club to accommodate the Cruising Association's members. And a short distance further east all our old friends who had lived in Brightlingsea Buildings were being rehoused elsewhere, as the whole block was due to be pulled down except for the tiny pub, the Black Horse, at one end. A row of ugly modern town houses arose in its place, soon to be occupied by suitable tenants for the new vibrant Narrow Street. Many of them had varied and interesting backgrounds, but we bitterly missed some of the so-called problem families who had kept a friendly eye on us for all those years; even a woman who was known by her neighbours as GBH (Grievous Bodily Harm), as she had floored a 'Pig' (a policeman) on one occasion, much to the admiration of all and sundry!

All of a sudden the 'débris', which had long been the playground of the children from Brightlingsea Buildings as well as John Sharkey with his dog, was fenced in with thick barbed wire railings. The remaining Cockney residents, however, soon overcame that setback by forging a small entrance at the far end of Ropemakers Fields. But they could not repel the army of bulldozers which rapidly

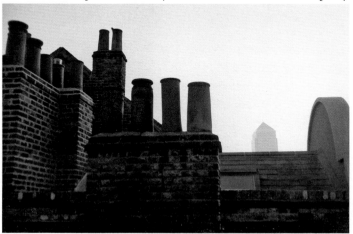

Lucy (slightly obscured), George, Doris and Albert (the chimney pots) with Canary Wharf in the background.

Bich Ha and her son, Philip, with our dog Tito out on the West India Docks.
arrived on the site.

The Limehouse Link Tunnel was to run beneath our patch, and during the months to follow a metal bridge was built across the churned-up morass where we used to hold our Guy Fawkes's parties; and a number of archaeology students discovered ancient clay pipes and even some Roman coins in the sea of mud below the bridge. There was a small hut occupied by a solemn bridge-keeper at one end, but he never failed to save half his lunch to give to our dog whenever we passed that way.

The most extraordinary building gradually arose to the east of us, on the Isle of Dogs. The West India Docks had originally consisted of several strips of water separated by tongues of land supporting custom-houses and cargo sheds, etc. After the banana-ships stopped calling there to pick up their passengers, it became 'free territory'. We kept our dinghy nearby, and I used to take some of the boys from Cyril Jackson School out sailing in her; and my Chinese friend, Bich Ha Mac, and her little boy, Philip, sometimes came too. Then, quite suddenly, the West India Docks were no longer 'free territory'. A pair of Canadian millionaires took possession of our favourite strips of water, and on a solid piece of land between them they quickly erected an immense building with a pointed roof which they called Canary Wharf. You could see it from miles away and it had a splendid display of multi-coloured lights near the summit at night.

* * * * * *

The arrival of Canary Wharf heralded the growth of a mini-Oxford Street beneath it, and many offices and business premises above and all round it. The work-force came mainly from the City of London and further west, and the children of the original Isle of Dogs inhabitants found only a few openings on offer. When they married and

Canary Wharf from the Mudchute Farm.

Lunch at the Prospect of Whitby on Cissie's 90th birthday.

wished to buy a home of their own near where their families lived, it had become far too expensive, so they were forced to move to the outer suburbs, far away from the glittering prospects around Canary Wharf.

Some of our old acquaintances were luckier than others; or maybe their children worked harder at school, and achieved exam results which opened up new and exciting futures for them. The Wapping gang, my first friends from way back in the 1940s, have remained good friends ever since. Some of us meet at the Prospect of Whitby every December for our annual Christmas party, and we celebrated Cissie's 90th birthday there not so long ago. She was Lucy's last remaining daughter.

Junie, one of Lucy's grand-daughters, (we used to meet in the Kentish hop fields long ago), moved with her husband, Tommy Knock, and their son, Anthony, to a nice house near Romford; and Anthony now works in the latest branch of Barclays Bank in Canary Wharf – somewhere high up in the sky.

Mrs Woodward Fisher's Barge Yard was sold to a rich property tycoon by her son, soon after her death; and he has turned it into three large flats with a fancy exterior which in no way resembles a working barge yard. Each flat was priced at more than half a million pounds, but the sound of the barges thundering together when a fast ship passes our windows had gone for ever. It seemed a far cry from the days when George and his work-force kept a sharp look-out for any strangers who found their way into our part of Narrow Street. Number 92A, which used to be the Woodward Fisher's engine workshop, was bought by a well-known East End boxer, Dennis Booty, and transformed by him and his wife, Maureen, into a very popular wine-bar. In recent years it has come under the brilliant management of John Fell and his hard-working team of boys and girls, many of whom have become good friends of ours and look after us well.

John Doble, the young man from the Foreign Office

Our house is the blue one and Booty's wine bar is two houses from the left.

who used to go to work in his dinghy or his little yellow German car, rose steadily in the ranks until he became British Ambassador in Swaziland. He was determined, however, to keep his house in Narrow Street, formerly below the shadow of Limehouse Lil; so he rents it to travelling journalists from the Daily Telegraph during his long absences abroad.

John's latest adventure – he has now retired from the Foreign Office – was to follow in the footsteps of a friend he made in Swaziland who is the only black African ever to reach the summit of Mount Everest. And John, although he has had no training as a mountaineer himself, struggled to a point not far from the summit of the fourth highest mountain in the Himalayas, before the weather suddenly changed and ruined his chances.

Jack and Renie retired from The Grapes and went to live in their holiday home in Broadstairs, about the same time as Mr Watts, the vicar of St Anne's Church, moved to a small parish in the Welsh mountains. He died there a few years later, but his widow often returned to visit her old home in Limehouse.

Various landlords took over The Grapes, until Barbara Haigh arrived on the scene. She was a bunny-girl in her youth, and she rules her little corner of Narrow Street with

Above: Lucky with his wife, Joanne, and eldest son, Luke, paying us a visit at Christmastime.

a firm hand and a lovely sense of humour.

The Indian family of Mr Lal Singh who grew up in Brightlingsea Buildings, increased by three more children after Sheila's arrival in London. The family moved to Stratford later on, but we kept in touch with them whenever possible. Lucky and his sister, Rani, had always been our special friends; and we were invited to Rani's wedding, our first Indian wedding, in which the bride, who had not been allowed to choose her husband-to-be, shed many bitter tears on the great day. Later on, however, she came to visit us with her husband and first baby, and she seemed very happy and contented.

Dick knew that Lucky was devoted to an English girl whom he had met on holiday on the East Coast, so he had a serious talk with Lal and persuaded him to allow his son to marry her. They settled down in Ipswich, and Lucky found a good job in the port of Felixstowe. In due course they had two sons, Luke and Adam, and the marriage has been a great success. Every Christmas Lucky and Joanna and their two boys come to London to visit his family and us.

John Sharkey, the Irish tramp, was offered a council flat in a large block close to the East India Dock Road some while after J.B.Riney and Co. had moved to other

Rani and her little boy and our dog Tito.

parts of London. He accepted it with pride, but it turned out to be a sad choice. How could a man who had enjoyed most of his life on the open road, surrounded mainly by his fellow-countrymen, live inside a huge dark building and close his front door to the world outside? And then there were all the worries of keeping the place clean, paying the rent and rates and electricity bills etc.; and how to cope with snooty disagreeable neighbours, and what to do with all the spare time with which he was lumbered?

We called to see him once or twice, but poor John was inconsolable, and his only companions were a pair of nuns from a Catholic church nearby who tried to care for him as best they could; and he had an occasional visit from Michael Collins, a boy who had lived in Brightlingsea Buildings at the same time as John was living in his little wooden hut in Narrow Street.

After a year or two John had reached the end of his tether. The nuns and priests from the Catholic church arranged for him to go home to Ireland, to a care home for the elderly close

Above: Dick dancing with the crowd during the London Marathon, which passes our house.

to his birthplace where he had spent much of his childhood.

When Canary Wharf was up and flourishing, some of the old buildings at the eastern end of Narrow Street were scheduled for demolition, including Garford House where our Chinese family lived. Several of them had married other Chinese boys or girls by then, and The Ngoc and Quan Anh with some of their children and grandchildren were moved to Timber Wharves on the Isle of Dogs. Attractive houses with their own small gardens had been built close to the Millwall Dock, and Bich Ha with her husband and four children found themselves living next-door to her parents and only a short distance from two or three of her sisters. Many of the menfolk had good jobs in Chinese restaurants nearby, and Thai Ha and her husband, Simon, ran their own restaurant in Hornchurch for a while, until they were made almost bankrupt by the Hong Kong business man who lent them money to start with. Simon now has an important position aboard the Lotus Restaurant, a magnificent floating establishment in the

Maxine Nhin playing our grand piano at Butterfields.

219

West India Docks. Thai Ha works at Asda near the Mudchute Farm, and they have two little girls, Maxine and Jade. Maxine is fast becoming a talented pianist.

The Chinese children usually work hard at school, which is why they often get good jobs when they grow up; then they save much of their earnings so that they have the chance to buy their own homes and become independent citizens.

Another family from the old buildings, Peter, Johnny and Vera Roberts, whose parents died soon after their move to Dagenham, have always remained 'best friends' of ours. They never forget our birthdays nor Christmastime; and not a year passes without Peter and his brother and sister arriving at the Prospect of Whitby for our Christmas party with a trolley full of lovely presents and a hamper bursting with nourishing food and drink. They have never owned a car, but somehow they manage to transport all those treasures from Dagenham by bus and on foot, no matter how bad the winter weather might be.

"We want to keep an eye on you; make sure you don't

Dick's birthday breakfast.

go short of nothing in the cold winter days, see what I mean?" Peter explains, heaving his trolley up the steep staircase inside the pub.

These are only a few of the people who have done so much to brighten up our lives in this magic corner of the East End. Then there are all the famous people: writers, artists, actors, film-producers, journalists, politicians, etc., who have lived in and around Narrow Street. Andrew Sinclair, who sold us Number 88, was responsible for buying the row of houses from The Grapes to the Barge Yard, then selling them to his friends from Cambridge before the demolition squads moved in. David Owen arrived there only a few months before us; and when his life story "Time to Declare", was published several years later, he wrote on the fly-leaf of his present to us; "Dick and Rozelle, With best wishes to our best neighbours, David Owen".

Daniel Farson, the son of Negley Farson, who ran a famous pub on the Isle of Dogs and wrote some memorable books, was another close neighbour. The painters, Teddy Wolfe and Francis Bacon, the wonderful actor Ian McKellen, the journalist Matthew Parris; and Janet Street-Porter (right next-door), who made short work of three husbands during her stay alongside us!

We are still here, at Number 88. And we have had no desire to get in touch with Andrew Sinclair and warn him that we are thinking of leaving – despite the fact that life on the Narrow Street side of our house seems quite different now. A constant stream of sparsely-clad runners, building their expertise for the next London Marathon, pass from right to left and left to right – we have to be careful each time we emerge from our front door. Then there are the smartly-dressed "Yuppees" with mobile phones clamped to their faces and staccato jokes being exchanged with friends at work in Canary Wharf. Jazzy sports cars flash by, and the Bangladeshi children from the tower blocks overlooking the new little park regard the scene with interest and speculation.

A powerful Sun tug blows her siren to announce the arrival of her charge – a mighty ocean liner – on the river side of our house. She is followed by a packed-tight pleasure-launch returning from Greenwich, a pair of Dutch sailing-yachts and another smaller tug, towing a string of lighters. Her skipper is an old friend of ours – Peter Duggan (related to Lucy Durrell's family from Wapping).

I hang out of the ground floor window revelling in the waves that come galloping towards our house; and suddenly I remember that Merchant Navy bloke sweltering in a waterfront bar in Calcutta, who growled "Gawd fer a whiff of Li'mus Reach!".

And a chirpy kind of voice behind him said "Amen".

Limehouse Reach at dawn, from our bedroom window, looking downriver towards Greenwich.

Other books by Rozelle Raynes

Each book is fully illustrated with photographs and the author's own drawings

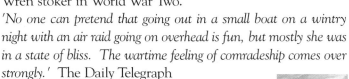

MAID MATELOT
This is the third edition of a book where Rozelle Raynes relates her adventures as a Wren stoker in World War Two.

'No one can pretend that going out in a small boat on a wintry night with an air raid going on overhead is fun, but mostly she was in a state of bliss. The wartime feeling of comradeship comes over strongly.' The Daily Telegraph
ISBN 0954746708   paperback   £6.99

THE TUESDAY BOYS
The story of eight boys from East London who grew up together in Care, and their adventures aboard Rozelle Raynes' Folkboat 'Martha McGilda' as she taught them all about sailing.

'A book which will delight and entertain...and it will move the reader deeply.' Yachting Monthly
ISBN 1871482062   hardback   £10.95

A BOAT CALLED MARTHA
Rozelle Raynes vividly describes over forty years of sailing 'Martha McGilda'.

'Will entrance all lovers of sailing and boats. In fact, the author's sheer delight in what she does and her wonderful way with words makes this a very enjoyable book for all readers, even for non sailors.' The Wren
ISBN 1900289474   hardback   £15.00

27 KISSES

The Last Coach from Croatia

A unique, true story of four homeless families from the former Yugoslavia who escaped to England, and of how the author and her husband made a home for them. A moving and frequently amusing tale narrated in the author's usual highly descriptive and personal style.

ISBN 1871482143   paperback   £7.95

All available to order from bookshops or direct from Thoresby Gallery, Thoresby Park, Ollerton, Newark NG22 9EP (telephone 01623 822465/822009) or email gallery@thoresby.com. If ordering from Thoresby Gallery cheques should be made payable to Thoresby Gallery. Credit/debit cards accepted. If paying by cheque please add £2.50 for postage and packing regardless of how many books ordered. Thank you. For card payments £2.50 will be added to your transaction.